The Church in Cornwall

The Church in
Cornwall
H Miles Brown

Introduction by Joanna Mattingly

Cornish Classics No 6

First published 1964 Oscar Blackford Ltd
This edition published by Cornish Classics 2006

Cornish Classics is an imprint of Truran Books Ltd
Croft Prince, Mount Hawke, Truro, Cornwall TR4 8EE
www.truranbooks.co.uk

Cover design by Peter Bennett, St Ives
Typeset by Kestrel Data, Exeter, Devon

Printed in Great Britain by
Short Run Press Ltd, Exeter, Devon

Contents

Introduction

SOME NINETEEN YEARS AGO I FIRST CAME ACROSS THIS SLIM book in Truro Bookshop. I purchased one of the last copies for a modest £3 and thereafter it provided the backbone for many church history classes. 'Here in a reasonable compass' as the then bishop of Truro wrote was something to whet the appetite, and it has certainly inspired me, and others, to look further into the subject of Cornwall's churches over the ensuing years. Dr Miles Brown writes with an enviable fluency and clarity of vision and this remains one of the most readable books of its type. It is now over forty years since its first publication and the book has achieved classic status.

As will be seen, many of the ideas that were current in 1964 have now been discredited or superseded. Advances in scholarship and archaeology are largely responsible and the present reader is referred to C Thomas and J Mattingly, *The History of Christianity in Cornwall AD 500–2000* (2000) for a more up-to date reading list. *Unity and Variety: A History of the Church in Devon and Cornwall*, edited by Nicholas Orme in 1991 perhaps comes closest to supplanting H Miles Brown's *The Church in Cornwall*, and could be read along-side. However, unlike *The Church in Cornwall*, *Unity and Variety* is the work of many authors rather than one.

Interest in Cornish church history continues to flourish. Recent research projects under the wing of the Institute of Cornish Studies have included a comparison of medieval Cornish lantern crosses with those of Somerset, sixteenth and seventeenth century slate Cornish-made tombstones, the early Quakers, and church rearrangement in the twentieth centuries.

The Church in Cornwall comprised a mere 120 pages when first published – an amazing feat of succinctness. This is all the more remarkable as it included further reading, places to see, and an index. It also epitomised the age it was written in – an age of ecumenicalism and reconciliation, especially with the Catholic church. Miles Brown wrote 'as an Anglican . . . in as impartial a frame' as was possible. He was vicar of St Winnow and St Veep from 1962 and later became a Canon of Truro Cathedral. Among his friends and associates were the eminent Methodist historian, the Reverend Tom Shaw, and Dr A.L. Rowse. I particularly remember Miles Brown's humorous but affectionate vote of thanks following a lecture by Rowse on the history of Lostwithiel and A.L.'s roars of appreciative laughter. I also remember with gratitude the help Miles Brown generously gave me during the preparation of a major Civil War exhibition held at the Royal Cornwall Museum in 1992. Ten years later it was an idea of Pat Brown, Miles Brown's widow that led to the *Treasures of the See* exhibitions in Truro Cathedral. These commemorated the one hundred and twenty-fifth anniversary of Truro Diocese throughout 2002 and enabled Christine North and myself to explore the parts of churches that architectural historians never reach, including flower arrangers cupboard, in search of treasures and curiosities.

Miles Brown's aim in *The Church in Cornwall* was to tell the story of the 'rise and development of the faith and the story of church and chapel' in Cornwall. From the appearance of the three British bishops at the Council of Arles in 314 to the state of the church in his own day, he strove to sort historic fact from myth. The 'whole calendar of Methodist saints' or 118 branches of the Mother's Union in 1962 are considered as worthy of study as the 'Celtic' saints and medieval guilds. There is a refreshing honesty here and the book reveals much of the man. Other views are tolerated to some extent and occasionally the romantic viewpoint triumphs temporarily over the academic. Another aspect that adds to the books charm is Miles Brown's passion for Cornwall, a place where 'religion is a topic to be taken seriously'. However, it is the stories, many of which conjure up visual images, and Miles Brown's indomitable sense of humour, that really make this book a classic for me.

The book begins with a chapter on the Celtic church – a concept now largely discredited and rewritten by Charles Thomas, Oliver Padel and others. Druids and Joseph of Arimathea are given short shrift as part of 'pious imagination' but the door is not fully closed. While accepting that the 170 or so Cornish saints may be 'unhistorical persons', Miles Brown prefers, like many today, to believe that it is possible to really walk in their footsteps. He also describes Tintagel as a monastic site – a view then current, and would like to believe that May day at Padstow and Helston 'may be survivals of not-so-innocent customs of a pre-Christian age . . .'. In the former case, Tintagel is now seen as a seasonal royal court and not a monastery at all and in the latter, origins before the early sixteenth century are unlikely.

The Medieval (Catholic) church covers a broad swathe from the proto-bishops before the Norman Conquest to Thomas Vyvian, prior of Bodmin, who became bishop of Megara in 1517 'as if Cornwall once again had its own bishop'. The new Victoria County History study of Cornish religious houses by Nicholas Orme is likely to dispel the idea of a 'happy-go-lucky sort of monasticism dear to the Celtic mind'. Similarly excavations at Glasney and the discovery of the play Beunans Ke have helped reinstate Glasney as one of the five major Cornish religious houses. Dendrochronology (tree ring dating) at Miles Brown's old church of St Veep is set to revolutionarise our understanding of the rebuilding of Cornish churches. The south aisle at St Veep is now thought to be no earlier than the 1460s and the north probably dates from the 1540s. The majority of Cornwall's churches appear to have undergone major remodelling (or the final phases of it) in the period 1520s-40s not in the fifteenth century – Bodmin, and St Kew may be among the exceptions. Where Miles Brown's contribution remains most valid is in setting Cornwall in the context of Exeter diocese and showing that the personalities of bishops and clergy really did matter.

'The Reformation so disastrous, so splendid . . .' and the Commonwealth is the chapter that first highlights Miles Brown's scholarship and skill in using documentary sources. The flood of church land that benefited so many Cornish landowners is set against the execution of the vicars of St Veep and Poundstock for their part in the 1549 rebellion. National history provides the context but there is much about the people involved here too – poor bishop Turberville of Exeter who refused to give up his Catholicism and was lodged in the Tower of London. Perhaps surprisingly, in view of the Catholicism of the county, only six parish priests followed his lead and were deprived in 1559. The idea that the 'sonorous liturgy . . . speeded the retreat of the Cornish language' is still at the centre of debate. Devout clergy like the nonagenarian Hugh Atwell of St Ewe who prescribed 'milk, apples, and fresh air' to sick parishioners inhabit the pages leading up to the Civil War – another of Miles Brown's passions. The loss of the tower of the chapel of St Nectan in St Winnow and the story of the baptism of a horse as 'Charles' in the font of Lostwithiel church are to be found in this section of his book. JP-controlled marriages in the Commonwealth period led to the bemused comment in the Launceston parish register about 'the profanes[s] and giddiness of the times'.

The fourth chapter focuses on the Restoration and the eighteenth century beginning with the triumphal entry in 1660 of the new bishop of Exeter with coaches and thousands of horses. Among his first tasks were the demolition of the 'Babylonish wall' in the cathedral (like those erected in St Giles, Edinburgh to create more manageable preaching boxes) and the conversion of a sugar refinery back into a bishop's palace. We are presented with the 'dowbaked' Puritan parishioners of Kilkhampton who objected to their Grenville incumbent wearing a surplice. The reintroduction of organs (another subject close to Miles Brown's heart as he built the organ now at Caerhays) took place at Falmouth as early as 1702 and Launceston in 1723. The sacrifice of Madron's rood screen in 1751 for a performance of a Handel oratorio shows the practical motivation behind so much Georgian vandalism of earlier church fabric. Meanwhile James III was proclaimed king in St Columb Major market place in 1714 and John Wesley's first visit coincided with another Jacobite scare in 1743. The achievements in science and culture of eighteenth century clergy are rightly extolled, and who could forget Reverend Whitaker of Ruan Lanihorne's ebony false teeth?

One of the most fascinating sections is chapter 5, which covers 'the Separations' from the Anglican church. Starting with the Roman Catholics and the papal 'roaring bull' of 1570 which excommunicated Queen Elizabeth I on grounds of illegitimacy and made Catholics into reluctant traitors and recusants, the story concludes with the 1850 appointment of a Roman Catholic bishop at Plymouth. Presbyterians and Congregationalists 'illegal up to 1689' come next with their farmhouse and urban based conventicles and meeting houses. The section on Baptists starts with the possible sea baptism c1650 of the governor of St Mawes' daughter and concludes with Theodore Robinson, son of a Falmouth Baptist, who wrote on Jewish culture. Quakers are set in context and their contribution 'out of all proportion to their numbers' in the field of commerce acknowledged. Finally Later Methodism is tackled, after 1791 when the death of Wesley severed the association with the Anglican Church. The role of female preachers here and in the other Separations is noted.

The sixth and last chapter focuses on the Anglican revival which began in 1833 and we have a visual picture of the hen-pecked Reverend Hoblyn of Mylor in 1831 to set against the well-known bearded figure of later photographs. Congregationless churches are nothing new as Bishop Phillpotts noted at St Ives at this time. Insights into church building include Pendeen where Reverend Aitken made templates of newspaper and stuck them on to beach boulders c1848. The return of colour and music could enflame the descendants of the 'dowbaked' Kilkhamptonians, or inspire the clerical Willimotts of this world. Sometimes it was also a clash of personalities that led to disputes, thus Miles Brown noted that Gorham (the author of a book on St Neot), vicar of St Just-in-Penwith, was reported to his bishop because 'he don't like we, and we don't like he!' Restorations got better towards the end of the nineteenth century, and in 1895 there were still remnants of 18 church bands. An account of the foundation of the new see will also be found here as well as the ritualist disputes focused on candle-counts at places like Porthleven, Cury and St Hilary, which by the 1920s-30s were getting more violent. Nothing seems to escape Miles Brown's broad overview. Fallen women's homes have a place here, and the book concludes with a statistical analysis of the church in 1962.

Joanna Mattingly
1 March 2005

Foreword

WHETHER WE ARE WELCOMING OR WRESTLING WITH THE
Report of Anglican Methodist Conversations, or rejoicing
in the new friendliness of attitude, and in some quarters of
approach, on the part of the Roman Catholic Church, we
shall find Canon Miles Brown's book a real help.

Though our times and personalities may seem to us so
different from those of the Wesleys – or the recusants – it is
important that we should know the historical background
and the not always religious reasons for our separatenesses.

Here in a reasonable compass – so helpful in these
days of unwillingness or inability to refer to the longer
history books – we are given a record which includes so
much that we need to know about, in a proper perspective
and with encouragement to learn it.

I do commend this short but comprehensive History of
our County and Diocese – with admiration and gratitude
for the author's learning and skill in making it available for
us.

Maurice Truron

Preface

IN CORNWALL CHRISTIAN ROOTS GO DEEP AND WIDE. Century upon century of faith and worship have left mark and sign upon village, moor and hill. From any vantage point in the county the towers of our churches will be seen sturdy and grey against the pleasant green of field and tree, or the brown hues of rocky outcrops. The starker outlines of the village chapel will not be far away, and in outlying parts the chapel keeps company with the ruins of old engine houses once the scene of enterprise and faith.

Talk to the people of the land and you will find religion is a topic to be taken seriously. Not for the Cornishmen are the fashionable agnostic platitudes common nowadays. The place given to religion may lead the individual Celt to pasture in strange regions such as Mormonism, or to little bethels standing alone unconnected with any similar groups, but its importance is unquestioned.

What is the history of Christianity in Cornwall? This book sets out broadly the rise and development of the faith, and tells the story of church and chapel in the hope that greater understanding of 'what God hath wrought' will result. It is inevitable that the main emphasis will be on the worship and activity centring on the old parish churches of the county, but the various denominations of the more usual kind will also share in the telling. If any belonging to these find anything herein which gives offence, it is not so intended. I write as an Anglican, but in as impartial a frame as I can, and my purpose is to make clear the course of events which has led to things as they are today.

This book makes no claim to be more than an outline introductory to the history of the Christianity of Cornwall. Readers will no doubt wish to turn to the well-known detailed studies of the Celtic Age, the medieval period, Tudor Cornwall, and the county during the Civil War after they have read the present work. The dependence of the earlier part of this book on such larger studies is obvious and is acknowledged with gratitude. The later chapters herein, however, tell much which has not been set out before in order and students of Cornish history may profit from them, and from the whole story as presented in outline form.

Visitors, teachers, and churchpeople generally, it is hoped, will find their knowledge of Cornwall and its churches enriched by this book, and there may well result a desire to explore some of the places mentioned. The list of interesting churches and relics of the past will be useful to those arranging school parties and outings.

Many friends have helped me in gathering material for this book over a long period, and I would acknowledge my debt to them. In particular I am grateful to Mr. Ashley Rowe and to Canon J. H. Adams for reading the typescript and offering advice and criticism from their wide knowledge of Cornish matters, to Rev. T. Shaw, of the Cornish Methodist Historical Association, and others for the loan of books. I also owe much to Mr. H. L. Douch, the Curator of the County Museum, for his interest and readiness to assist.

H. Miles Brown
St. Winnow, 1964

1

The Celtic Church

NO ONE WHO WOULD WISH TO UNDERSTAND THE INSTITU-
tions of the nation and the formation of its character can
afford to neglect the story of the Church in these islands.
To the Christian, in addition, the religion he professes is
bound up with it, and he sees in its growth and development signs of the promised guidance of the Spirit in its
constant renewal and triumph over human frailty and error.

The story of Christianity in Cornwall is something
more than that of the whole in miniature. The county is an
area distinct, not only in geographical bounding by the sea.
It is distinct in the contribution it made and makes to the
complex whole – an enthusiasm ascetic and individualistic
in Celtic days; a resistance to change at the time of Reform;
a more wholehearted loyalty to king and Church at the
time of the Civil War; a fervent welcome to Wesley, with
a whole calendar of Methodist saints; a mighty Church
revival and a new cathedral. And so we might go on.

Yet as a proportioned whole the story is unknown to
the vast majority of Cornishmen. Some periods, as of the
medieval church or the coming of Wesley, have been
studied minutely. Here however will be found only an
outline, but an outline of the Church's progress in every
century up to the present. Some parts of this story have
never been told before.

The antiquity of the Christian faith in this land is often quite unrealized, and not only by the modern visitor speeding by in his car. Yet the evidence lies around for those who can read it. It meets us at the end of a lane to the sea, in a few stones remaining from an ancient place of prayer; on the bleak moorland track, with an old granite cross, or in the tumbled walls of the medieval chapel of a great house.

The inhabitants of Cornwall to whom the first unknown missionaries came had long been settled in the land. They were the most western representatives of a group of tribes of mixed race, possibly loosely confederated, and spread over Wiltshire, Somerset, Dorset, Devonshire and Cornwall. Known as Dumnonii, they have given their name to Cornwall's neighbour county on the east.

By the time of the invasion of the Romans, a.d. 43, the Dumnonii had been pressed back by other tribal settlers into isolation in the two counties of Devon and Cornwall, cut off from their allies in the Severn basin and beyond. It may well have been that the new invasion from Gaul was not unwelcome to the Dumnonii, and that they willingly accepted the status of a client kingdom to Rome. No clear evidence appears that the Roman conquerors proceeded in force west of the Exe. Here a new capital, Isca Dumnoniorum (Exeter) was founded.

The few undoubted Roman remains discovered in Cornwall give us a picture of a loosely-held region, with a superficial penetration sufficient to give control over the tin trade and the tracks over which the commerce of the area travelled to the sea.

The inhabitants in the first century of the Christian era would seem to have been a peaceful people with a degree of culture. Their houses were often two or three rooms grouped around a courtyard, as can be seen at Chysauster (from the first to third centuries a.d.), and constructed of stone, circular in form, surmounted by a conical roof of poles and reed thatch. Advantages had come to the people by reason of the trade in tin, and there are signs of the exportation of gold, silver and iron. In return they received such luxuries as glass, ivory, pottery and amber fashioned into necklaces and bracelets. Some of this culture would derive by way of imitation of that of the Roman overlords. There is near Camborne the trace of a small villa in the Roman style, in which can be seen the local interpretation of what might have been familiar to some official who had served time in more sophisticated regions.

It might be asked – what was the religion of the Cornish at this time, and on what principles did they control their lives? An earlier age – that of Borlase in the eighteenth century – saw everywhere the influence of the Druids. Every worn stone or standing menhir, barrow or other feature was attributed to these ancient priests, and on this basis speculation ran riot as to the bloody rites which had been carried on in times past.

It seems likely that the people of these shores shared the primitive and widespread belief in a religion of nature, the possession by spirits of stones and the deep recesses of the forests then more common in Cornwall. They would no doubt venerate the springs upon which their life depended, and the fires which kept them warm in winter. Some of the ancient rites which remain in an innocent form, such as the May revels at Padstow and Helston, may be survivals of not-so-innocent customs of a pre-Christian age, for these things are often long adying.

In the 'Lives' of the Saints we hear of the inhabitants of the day worshipping crude images of deities. Fear, insecurity and superstition were part of everyday life, and the doctrines of the new faith, coupled with the boldness and ascetic lives of its missionaries were undoubtedly powerful to attract disciples.

But when was the Gospel first preached in these parts?

Pious imagination, making the most of silences in the New Testament accounts of Our Lord's life, and the undoubted gaps in history, has given rise to legends of the visits of Joseph of Arimathea, St. Paul, and even Jesus himself, in childhood days, to Cornwall.

Beautiful though some of these tales are, they belong more to devotional speculation than to historical fact. There is no evidence which actually contradicts them, so no doubt they will continue to have a hold on the minds of some. More probably they represent a personalization of the coming of faith in Christ in the preaching of merchants and soldiers converted on the continent.

Real evidence of the Church's presence in the first four Christian centuries is scanty in the extreme. We know that at the Council of Arles in 314 there were three bishops present from Britain, and that they were poor, being unable unassisted to bear the cost of travel. We do not know for certain that they came from Cornwall of course; Wales or some other region might equally have been their place of origin.

The first undoubted traces of a small Christian community in Cornwall are found in the area of the Hayle estuary. There is an inscribed stone at Carnsew which shows Christian influence and may be dated 350–450, and a small stone of the same period bearing the Chi-Rho monogram – a Christian symbol without doubt – is to be found at Phillack in the same district.

From the 'Life' of St. Fingar or Gwinear we learn that the band of missionaries who came with him and St. Piala found not far from the shore at Hayle a cell inhabited by a holy virgin. This cell may well have been on the site of a medieval chapel on the rock known as Chapel Anya. Also from an early period are the remains of monastic cells on the island at Tintagel, the earliest of which may have been built about 350.

The most we can say is that by the time the Roman

14

occupation came to an end in the middle of the fifth century some few centres may have been Christianized, centres probably scattered and to be found at the estuaries of rivers convenient for travel by sea to Gaul, to Ireland, and to Wales.

The drawing back of the Roman military power left a vacuum. One great unifying force was found in Christianity. The whole region, now unprotected by the legions, lay open to raids from oversea, and from about 428 the Saxons began their efforts to overrun the land. Far from the life of the Continent, the western region was soon cut off, and there emerged a kind of Celtic community or loose series of communities in Ireland, Wales and Cornwall with a common outlook, language and religion.

The effect of the Saxon raids was to press the inhabitants of Britain, till then more or less integrated with Cornwall and Wales, into the western fringe. The invading Saxons were at that date pagan, and the tendency was for the British refugees to adhere fanatically to their newfound faith, and to the relics of their Roman background, and cherish them in the isolation of the distant shores of the Celtic lands. From Cornwall a great number crossed into Brittany, which derives its name from this migration. The 'Age of the Saints' was about to begin, and its fascinating story must be set against the background of this isolation, the defence against the continuous invasions of Danes and Saxons, the sting of the salt seas and the sound of the wind in the seaways between the Celtic lands.

Somewhere about the year 450 a large party of evangelists landed in the Phillack district. Their point of departure is taken to be either Ireland or Wales, and they were accompanied by Gwinear and Piala. The local chief, Teudor, was not unnaturally disturbed by this 'invasion'; the 'Life' of St. Gwinear says there were 770 men and seven bishops in the party! Teudor gathered his soldiers and attacked the mission from behind. All in one day were thus made martyrs for Christ, including Gwinear, slain at Roseworthy, who is reckoned as the protomartyr of Cornwall.

Befittingly, several miracles attributed to the intercession of the saint are recorded in the 'Life'. Like most of these saintly 'Lives', however, this was written many centuries after the time of the hero it describes.

In spite of the apparently limited opportunities for evangelization Gwinear and his companions evidently left some trace of their witness. The names of the two chief martyrs, Gwinear and Piala, came to be given to adjoining parishes; later fashion substituted the better-known Felicitas for the obscure female Piala, at Phillack.

Contemporaneous with the emigration of Britons to Brittany, or Armorica, were other incursions of Irish or Welsh into Cornwall, bent on evangelizing the land. The twenty-four children of a Welsh king, Brychan, landed, it is said, on the north coast of Cornwall, and to this day the churches in that part bear their names as patrons. In the Meneage district, south of Helston, we find saints honoured whose names are also found in the parishes and calendars of Brittany – such as Melaine, Winwaloe, Corentin and Mawgan.

Obviously there was much coming and going in the estuaries and creeks of Cornwall, and to this day several churches of ancient foundation remain set by the tidal waters of some lovely valley or sheltered round a spur of cliff from the beat of the waves. St. Winnow, Ruan Lanyhorne, Gunwalloe, St-Just-in-Roseland, Landulph, St. John, and others will occur to the mind of those familiar with the county. No doubt it was the constant travelling by sea on lightly built coracles on the part of the saints, carrying their portable altars of stone which has given rise to the medieval tales of their floating on leaves, or millstones and other unlikely articles.

The Celtic regions are peculiar in preserving in their

place names the names of Christian pioneers and early pastors. Cornish villages sometimes share saints with places in Wales, and in Brittany. The cult or veneration which has attached itself to these ancient heroes was not the result of a formal canonization, for such at that time was everywhere unknown. The zeal and holiness, the ascetic practices and the tireless preaching journeys with staff and bell aroused the awe of converts and others of the district where the saint had his cell.

Altogether some 170 saints are honoured in Cornwall, though nearly half are but names to us at this distance of time. While there are some who would dismiss them all as unhistorical persons, this seems a rather desperate course, since in the light of modern scholarship basic facts can be discerned underlying the legendary accretions, enabling us to sketch in the background of their lives and labours.

The Celtic Church was monastic in its structure, in Cornwall as elsewhere. It was a loose kind of association of monks, far removed from the ordered, disciplined system we associate with the great monasteries of the Middle Ages. In the earliest days, no doubt, there would be the pattern of isolated hermitages, or groups of two or three such settlements, founded by the local 'saint'. With further disciples joining the saint in his devotion something like a community would come into being. The common Cornish prefix 'lan', found in such names as Landulph, Lanivet, Landewednack, Landrake, Lansallos and so forth has the meaning 'monastic enclosure'. In some simple form there may have been in each such place a little group of students gathered round some priest or teacher and living their lives under his ascetic rule and example.

In later days there might emerge the greater Celtic monasteries, in which the memory of the founder was venerated, and his name would be attached by his disciples to churches and wells in the regions where they preached. In these greater communities the unit would be the abbot, who was perhaps also a bishop, bearing the episcopal authority probably via Ireland or Gaul. The fame of the outstanding abbot-bishops attracted disciples, and their devotions and ascetic practices would make a great impression on the simple people of the region, their teaching, though perhaps not free from superstition, convincing many hearts.

In Cornwall the numbers around any well-known figure might reach a hundred, which is small compared with, say, the two thousand disciples traditionally found in the Welsh monastery at Bangor Iscoed. In Ireland and Wales surviving evidence would show that similar centres were nurseries of art, of missionary zeal, and of civilizing influences. There is no reason to suppose the smaller, less well-known Cornish communities were any different.

We can picture the scene in some remote corner of the region in the sixth century. There would be a group of beehive-shaped huts (the rectangular ones at Tintagel seem exceptional) surrounded by a stone enclosure, formed of stones picked up from the moor and piled without mortar. In the midst would be a little oratory of wood or perhaps of stone. Such a 'church' exists in ruined form at Perranporth, the 'Lost Church' of St. Piran. A well and a crudely carved granite cross would be within the enclosure. The huts are the cells of monks, who have come to study with the famous teacher and saint. He himself would be clad in a white tunic with a rough coat of fur over it, a wallet hanging by his side. In the wallet there would be a beautifully illuminated service book or psalter. He would carry a staff with a curved spade-like top, and a small bell formed of metal sheets bent round and riveted. To us his appearance would be grotesque by reason of the Celtic tonsure. The head was shaved in front of a line drawn from ear to ear, the hair hanging down long behind. He would also wear a long beard.

The rough stone oratory or wattle chapel built by the

saint in his lifetime, or piously erected after his death, would enshrine his relics, and his mode of teaching and his scholarship would be carried on by those who had associated themselves with his work while he was alive.

Such were the austerities of the enthusiastic Celts that the rule adopted by these men for themselves was often harsh. Little food, long periods of absolute fasting, and the recitation of the psalter while immersed up to the neck in some cold pool were common practice. The devotion and self-surrender of these heroes of the faith gave them a willingly conceded power over the semi-civilized dwellers in the neighbourhood. Gifts of cattle and of land were pressed upon them and in the later age a trace of worldliness crept in.

Where, we may ask, were the important Cornish monasteries? On the summit of the island or rocky peninsula on the north coast at Tintagel, near the remains of a chapel dating from Norman times, a series of ledges on the north-east side of the cliff will be seen. In these ledges are the remains of dry-built rectangular chambers and several rock-cut graves. Objects discovered here show that this was in fact a Celtic monastery settlement on the lines of those known in Wales and Ireland. The oldest structures at Tintagel may well be as early as 350, but the whole series would stretch over several centuries up to about 800. The bleak surroundings in winter, the isolation, and the grandeur of the natural scene would appear an attractive site to a Celtic community.

The name of St. Juliot, one of the sons of Brychan, is associated with this headland. He probably arrived about 500. By then the site had been deserted by its earliest occupants, and here he built his cell and a tiny oratory. In time a flourishing community established itself at this spot, which, by the extent of the building remains recently uncovered, must have lasted some time, though it was no longer existing by the time of the Domesday survey (1086).

Probably the Saxon conquest brought it to an end, though not necessarily a violent one. The name and memory of St. Juliot are still preserved in the churches of Lanteglos and St. Juliot.

From their prominence in later times we would imagine that Bodmin and St. Germans were important Celtic centres. The former is associated with the name of St. Petroc, and other Celtic saints. St. Germans perhaps owes its origin to a saint of a similar sounding name, which has become assimilated to the name of the famous bishop of Auxerre who came to England to help stamp out the Pelagian heresy, but who probably never entered Cornwall.

Of the Cornish saints, St. Petroc stands out as 'the chief of the saints of Cornwall' and his work, and the veneration given him, extended over Devon as well as Cornwall. Several parishes in Devon, more in Cornwall, and some in Wales, bear his name as patron and perhaps preserve an outline of his travels in their distribution.

About the middle of the sixth century there landed on the coast near Padstow (that is, Petrocstow, the Saxon form) a company of holy men from Wales bent on evangelizing the district. Petroc was their leader. He is described as of royal blood, and one who had gone to Ireland to study, and there embraced the monastic life. Now he had returned as an active missionary monk.

The inhabitants of this part of Cornwall were still only partially converted, but Samson, another saint, was already established, perhaps at Lelissick, where later stood a chapel dedicated to him. Also in the vicinity was bishop Wethinoc. These two welcomed Petroc, and on his suggesting that he joined them, made over their cell to him, Wethinoc asking that his name should be remembered there. Petroc stayed on in 'Lanwethinoc', the Celtic name for Padstow, for more than thirty years, during which time he travelled on missionary tours over the whole of Dumnonia. In his 'Life', written of course centuries after his death, Petroc is said to have travelled to Rome, to Jerusalem, and to India. These extensive journeyings are probably the reflection in later accounts of his western travels.

Many miracles are attributed to Petroc. On his first landing, thirsty harvesters desired him to cause a spring to flow to assuage their thirst. The saint obligingly consented, and the spring remains as evidence of the truth of this wonder! More valuable was Petroc's act in the converting to Christianity of Constantine, petty king of Cornwall, who was either a pagan or a formal Christian. Petroc sent him to make a three-year retreat at a spot near the seashore near Trevone Head. The bay is still called Constantine's Bay, and there are the remains of a church there.

The community Petroc founded remained a principal centre long after his death in June 564. At some time after, the seat of this monastery was transferred to Bodmin, though some authorities put the move in Petroc's lifetime. As there was a Danish attack on the little port of Padstow in 981, this may mark the time of the removal, but Padstow continued to be an important and sacred spot for the Celtic and medieval church in spite of the transference of the monastery.

Perhaps St. Piran rivals Petroc in fame, and his name and person appear a little more real to us through the survival to our day of his 'oratory'. According to the (largely legendary) 'Life' he was chained by an angry mob of heathen Irish to a millstone, and cast into the sea from a high cliff. The waves at once obligingly stilled, and on this unlikely granite craft Piran sailed peacefully to Cornwall! The busy modern holiday resort of Perranporth enshrines his name, and there are other place names which keep his memory fresh in the minds of the Cornish. Piran is the patron saint of the tin miners, and is said to have discovered the secret of smelting the ore. This is most unlikely, however, in view of the much more ancient evidence of previous use.

In the sand dunes near the modern town, under an ugly concrete protecting shell put there in 1909, are the remains of 'St. Piran's Oratory', deservedly still the centre of pilgrimage. It was probably erected after the death of Piran to protect his resting place, and to shelter his relics and the pilgrims who came to venerate them.

From this humble place of worship we can gain a clear idea of the little shrines which once were found where now stand graceful parish churches. Not all the Celtic churches, however, would have been of stone – many doubtless were of wood or wattle. For the dedication of these holy places it was sufficient that the holy man should decide the site, which would be near a well or spring for baptism, and there he would remain for forty days praying and fasting. At the end of this period the church would be regarded as dedicated and fit to be used as a place for preaching the Gospel and the celebration of the Eucharist.

The Celtic Church had its own peculiar usages, derived partly from its long isolation from the rest of Christendom, and partly from a strand of tradition which seems to bear a similarity to Eastern Church customs. These differences created suspicion and difficulty later on when Celtic and Saxon Christians confronted one another.

Here and there a Celtic, or supposedly Celtic altar remains, as at the site of the monastery at Tintagel, and possibly the slab now in Camborne church. These are of stone, as is usually the case in the Western Church at that date. Surviving fragments of service books from Wales and Ireland indicate a Latin service, and that the Eucharistic rite shows similarity with Gallican sources, which themselves are akin to Orthodox liturgies in some minor respects. With the recitation of the psalter, the celebration of the sacraments, and the tireless preaching journeys the saints of Cornwall filled their days, their fervour and individualistic touch giving the Church in these parts a flavour all its own.

One of the features of Cornwall which never fails to strike the eye of the visitor to the county is the plenitude of ancient carved stone crosses, which especially abound in the far west of the county. It is very commonly supposed that the Christian missionary saints adapted pagan stone symbols or idols to Christian use in the earliest age, afterwards making crosses themselves as part of their expression of faith. Only slight documentary evidence remains as to the origin of these crosses. In the 'Life' of St. Samson, which comes from a date reasonably near to the events which it describes, we hear how the saint while staying in the district round Padstow comes across some pagan Cornish worshipping a stone idol, no doubt a symbol of nature-worship. The saint having convinced them of their errors, has the idol destroyed, but marks with the sign of the cross another stone in the near vicinity. Here it is not the actual idol which is Christianized, but a stone till then unused.

Whatever the origin of the familiar cross symbol, with the round head and equal armed Greek cross, it was not long before it was used and accepted as a Christian sign. In late Celtic times sepulchral monuments were commonly in the form of a cross; they were also used as marks of a preaching place, sometimes where no church building could be set up, as guiding stones on holy ways, and so forth.

In fact, right up to the threshold of the Reformation these crosses were being erected. In 1427 Dr. Reginald Mertherderwa directed in his will that new stone crosses of the usual kind should be erected on the way to Camborne church to mark the points at which the bearers should rest and prayer be made. The provision of such a cross was thought to be beneficial to the soul of the donor. Near Tintagel is a cross of Saxon date with the inscription: 'Aelnat made this cross for his soul.'

Typical too of Celtic Cornwall is the holy well. Probably a numinous place long before the saint had made his residence near by, it became associated with his ministry and imbued with his sanctity. There are wells called by the names of saints venerated in Cornwall to the number of fifty and more, and these we generally find near the religious settlement or 'lan' founded by the man or woman whose name they bear. But there are also wells called after saints who could not possibly have had anything to do with Cornwall, such as St. Anne, St. Clare, St. George, St. Martin, Our Lady, and there is even in St. Minver parish a Jesus well.

Many wells have buildings over them, some of them being elaborate in design incorporating small chapels. St. Madron's well has a chapel, in ruins, 25 ft. by 16 ft. At St. Clether the chapel retains its altar, and finely restored protecting structures exist at Dupath and St. Cleer. These buildings, however, are medieval and so do not properly concern us here, though the wells they grace are older.

Of interest in connection with Celtic liturgical use is the book known as the Bodmin Gospels, the only Cornish monastic book which has survived. It contains the liturgical Gospels to be read at the Eucharist, and is dated at about the end of the ninth century. It belonged to the monastery at Padstow and indicates the Latin use there. But also of interest is the fact that this book, being of the Gospels and therefore regarded as most sacred, was used to record the freeing of slaves before the altar of St. Petroc. Something like 122 names are written in of those who were probably descendants of the slaves of Cornish chieftains. Most of the freed bear Cornish names, but twelve are Saxon, as are the names of 33 of the liberators. The witnesses are monks of St. Petroc, mostly with Cornish names. The work of freeing was obviously regarded as a benefit for the soul of the liberator. No doubt this treasured volume was transferred with the monastery when the move to Bodmin was made.

Further illustrating devotional customs at this latter part of the ninth century is the discovery of liturgical ornaments buried near St. Austell. At some time in this period when the raids by the Danes were unusually threatening some Cornish clergy, probably of a district near the coast, buried their church treasures in an old tin stream at Trewhiddle, not far from St. Austell. They never returned to claim it, and for centuries it lay hidden until in recent times the hoard was uncovered.

The items recovered are rings, brooches, a small box, coins of Mercian and Wessex kings, a number of silver straps, a small, plain, but beautiful chalice, and a silver wire scourge. This last item is unique among relics of past ages, but one cannot resist the feeling that its delicate workmanship must have been provided for an object purely ceremonial rather than for an actual 'discipline'.

The workmanship is clearly Saxon, showing that a good deal of that influence had penetrated to mid-Cornwall by the end of the ninth century. This indicates the march of events elsewhere which must now be considered.

In the year 597 an event had occurred which, while it was geographically remote from the west, was full of portent for the Celtic Church. In that year Augustine landed in Kent with the goodwill of the pope to begin the conversion of the heathen Saxon. He came, of course, with a background of the vigorous, self-confident, well-organized Church of the Continent, accepting and supporting the jurisdiction of the pope over the whole Church.

Before long he became aware of the reality of the differences between the Christianity he professed and that of the native Christians of the west. He had previously known of the existence of the British Church, and was to taste the difficulties inherent in reconciliation. At a conference with the British bishops at Augustine's Oak he invited them to adopt Catholic uses and to join in preaching to the heathen. They, supposing him to be arrogant, refused his plea and denied his authority.

The question of different uses remained unsolved. In

664 the Synod of Whitby was held, and representatives of both forms of observance attended. The matters under review were apparently trivial – the date of the observance of Easter, the form of the tonsure, and some matters relating to baptism. But under these trivialities lay a great matter. Was the Church of the British to go on its independent course, or was it to come under the influence, guidance and supremacy of the pope?

The decisions admitted the customs of the Roman Church and the abandonment of the peculiar Celtic features. But the Church of the west was not directly a party to them, and continued on its way. There was at that time still a pagan block between the Christianized Saxon east and the Celtic Dumnonia, and a direct confrontation seemed unlikely.

But the Saxons were pressing gradually westwards, and the Church now among them. About 705 Aldhelm, the abbot of Malmesbury, wrote to a king of Dumnonia named Geruntius, or Gerrans, urging him and his clergy to abandon the Celtic usage and come into line with the rest of Western Christendom. The response, though it does not survive in documentary form, is hardly in doubt. Perhaps Geruntius was able to hold the Saxons for a while, and with other petty kings engaged in battles with the invader, who made constant military raids on the county, but the end was in sight.

In 814 King Egbert rapidly passed through Cornwall on a harrying expedition, though he did not establish a permanent hold. A few years later the Cornish sought revenge by making a thrust towards Exeter, but their temerity was rewarded by their defeat at Gafulford – perhaps Camelford? Egbert thus became the first king of all England – but only for a short while.

The west bided its time. In the 830s a Danish fleet was off the coast of Cornwall. The restive Celts joined the Norsemen and prepared to expel the Saxons. Egbert was too quick for the unlikely allies, and in a battle at Hingston Down just by Callington, the Cornish and the Danes were truly routed. The Cornish renewed their allegiance, which they never again seriously broke. They were allowed their own native rulers for about a century after this defeat, since Egbert and his successors were busy in their turn holding back the Danes and so not inclined to interfere in Cornish matters. The English penetration halted north of the Bodmin moor. The Saxons settled themselves in the fertile lowlands, where they have left their place names.

Egbert, however, did one thing which humbled and impoverished the Celtic Church and brought it increasingly under Saxon influence. It has been mentioned that many gifts of land were made to the old monastic settlements, and Padstow, St. Petroc's own centre, was particularly rich with generous lands around Wadebridge and the northern coast. One of the acts of Egbert was to break up the countryside into large manors or estates. Three of these, which coincided with the old Church lands, he constituted strongholds and endowments of Saxon missionary enterprise among the Celts. These estates, as a later king explained in 909 to the bishop of Crediton, Eadulf, to whom he transferred them, formed centres 'from which year by year he might visit the Cornish people to extirpate their errors. For in times past, as far as possible, they resisted the truth and were not obedient to the apostolical decrees'. These three estates were Pawton (the lands of Petroc), Caellwic and Lanwithan. But Padstow town and its neighbourhood were allowed to remain in their old ownership of the monks of Petroc, and in medieval times became an important 'liberty'.

Any pretence at independence could not long be maintained. In or about 850 the Cornish bishop made his submission – possibly in the name of the whole Cornish Church – to Coelnoth, archbishop of Canterbury. The submission included the words:

> *Ego, Kenstec – ad episcopalum sedem in gente Cornubia in monasterio quod lingua Brittanum appelatur Dinurrin electus –*

Bishop Kenstec was thus bishop-elect of the monastery called Dinurrin, a bishop, that is, of the old sort, settled not in a diocese but in a monastery. Almost certainly Dinurrin is Bodmin, since in Petroc's day a saint by the name of Wron or Guron was resident there and his name would form the second syllable of the word Dinurrin. This suggestion fits the facts better than the other places which have been put forward as the original of the mysterious 'Dinurrin'.

The Danish threat to England was broken for a while by the time of Alfred and the uniting and civilizing of the country proceeded. By the time of Alfred's grandson, Athelstan, in 930, the people of Cornwall were brought truly under English rule. In dealing with the Church Athelstan was wise and firm. He formed a new diocese on the normal pattern for the Cornish, and set the seat at the Celtic monastery of St. German's in the east of the county in 931. This had the effect of putting the ecclesiastical centre far from the old axis – Padstow – Bodmin. But as a conciliatory gesture he appointed a Cornishman as bishop – Conan – who had no doubt accepted the 'apostolical decrees' of the Catholic Church.

One last struggle of the Cornish, in a rising by the chieftain Howell, brought Athelstan to the end of the county and to the Scillies. In thanksgiving for the successful putting down of the revolt Athelstan made a grant of land to the monastery settlement of St. Buryan 'free from all temporal taxation'. Thus favoured, no doubt the community had reformed itself on the new lines, and other monasteries would be encouraged to follow suit.

By the time of Athelstan's death, in 939, religious strife over Celtic differences had come to an end. The

Cornish petty kings were reduced to mere lords of the manor. In 994 a charter of Aethelred to bishop Ealdred of Cornwall gave him episcopal jurisdiction in the province of Cornwall 'that he may govern and rule his diocese – both the monastery and the domain of St. Petroc being under the control of him and his successors'.

2

The Medieval Church

AFTER CONAN THE CORNISHMAN A LINE OF SAXON BISHOPS
up to Burhwold in 1018 ruled the area once the field
of Celtic pioneering for the faith. In this, of course, there
was gain as well as loss, for Cornwall was brought once
more into the main stream of the life of the Church after
centuries of isolation which had fossilized old ways and
devotion.

Under the Saxons began the process by which the
old Celtic 'lans', or monastic settlements, were either
reconstituted or grouped, and many were abolished,
to provide endowment for the see and for new parochial
churches. It would appear that the familiar parochial
system, with its pastor responsible for the cure of souls in a
restricted area owed its origin to the reorganization of
the Church under the Saxons. This territorial system, so
different from the old Celtic amorphous grouping on a
tribal basis was no doubt long in settling in Cornwall. But
little by little the Celtic communities in many a Cornish
creek and coombe, served for generations by simple
independent Celtic monks and priests came to an end.

Instead, the parish church, associated with the manor
and its lord, with the priest tilling the land given him and
ministering to the souls of the parish, and a few larger
communities of monks under a stricter rule became more

usual, and during the time of the Normans the process of change would seem to have been completed.

The twenty years or so of Danish rule and supremacy hardly affected Cornwall, but it is recorded that Canute confirmed the gift of lands in Landrake and Landulph to the bishopric of St. Germans, to which also came the three estates of Pawton, Caellwic and Lanwithan in the time of Wulfsige, bishop about 970.

When Burhwold, the last of the St. Germans bishops, died in 1043 he was succeeded by his nephew Lyfing, who was at the time bishop of Crediton. This see had been founded in 909 for Devonshire. Lyfing held the two sees together for three years. On his death in 1046 Leofric was appointed to the united sees and the seat of the bishop was moved from Crediton to Exeter. Cornwall became in due course merely an archdeaconry in the diocese of Exeter and this state of things persisted until the formation of the see of Truro in 1876.

The lands, manors and property of the see of St. Germans, and lands once in the possession of communities founded by the great Cornish saints, passed into the ownership of the bishops of Exeter, who to the great majority of Cornishmen throughout the medieval period were remote and awful figures.

What of the simple people over whom the new bishops, set up by the Saxons, ruled? Some of our Christian forefathers of this period dwelt on the north Cornish coast near Mawgan Porth, and their village has been recently excavated, giving us a glimpse of their pattern of life across the centuries. This settlement was occupied from about the time of Egbert's conquest of Cornwall up to the eve of the Norman invasion. Grouped in a rectangular courtyard and protected by a low wall are several stone-built houses. The principal house was over thirty feet long. At one end was the byre, housing the cattle, in the middle of the main room was a cooking pit, and along the walls were slate bunks or beds. A cultivated plot terraced into the hillside showed some mastery of agriculture, and not far away was a cemetery where the bodies of their dead were placed in slate-lined graves, lying east and west in the Christian manner. It seems that the inhabitants were a peaceful pastoral people, familiar also with the sea and the art of fishing.

The coming of the Normans and the radical national reorganization they embarked upon involved a reformation of the Church. Cornwall naturally shared the experience of firmer rule, and new ideas in pastoral ministry and in building filtered down. The Saxon ways to the busy Normans must have seemed slack and inefficient, the clergy often little better than the peasants to whom they ministered. On the death of the Saxon Leofric Osbern was enthroned bishop of Exeter; he was, of course, a Norman.

The process, begun in Saxon times, of the reconstitution of Celtic monastic foundations continued. St. Michael's Mount was settled on the Benedictine rule and given to the Norman monastery of Mont St. Michel on the opposite coast of the Channel. The priory at Tywardreath was founded, also on Benedictine lines, before 1154. Minster, founded before 1190, was, like Tywardreath, given to the mother house of St. Sergius and St. Bacchus at Angers.

In the formation of parishes about one in three of the old Celtic holy places became the centres of new districts. The rest remained as places of minor pilgrimage, or chapels of ease, and later on some were adopted as domestic oratories when such became fashionable.

Lasting in its effect was the replacement of Celtic and Saxon church building by the more ambitious Norman structures. Much of the older building was in wood, or crudely-erected rubble with little or no mortar, as at St. Piran's Oratory. No undoubted remains of Saxon architecture survive, though some authorities recognize a pre-Conquest touch in the fonts at Morwenstow, Boyton and a few other places. But under the Normans an immense amount of building was begun, usually in a soft freestone as the working of native granite was yet but crudely done.

It is estimated that about 135 churches were built in Cornwall under the Normans. Traces of their work remain recognizably in many existing churches, though successive waves of enlargement and rebuilding have made them less obvious. By their size and dignity the new structures would no doubt appear magnificent in contrast with the little Celtic oratories or chapels of wattle, though to us the effect is dark and cramped. Notable for their Norman features are the churches at Tintagel, St. Breward, Morwenstow, Kilkhampton and Cury, among others.

Late in the Norman style is the church at St. Germans, under the Normans reconstituted as a college of Augustinian canons. Here they erected a grand church, of which the surviving parts, the twin tower bases, west door and arcade make it the finest example of the work of this period in the county. The canons of St. Germans were allowed to retain some part of the extensive estate which was once the property of the Cornish bishopric, and later on the gift of relics of St. Germanus of Auxerre stirred many pilgrims to visit and offer rich gifts to this church. This prosperity is reflected in the great edifice which can be seen today.

It was at this noble period of architecture that bishop William Warelwast, a nephew of William I, began the building of the twin towers, like Norman castle keeps, of Exeter cathedral. It was Warelwast who settled the priories of Bodmin and Launceston on the basis of Augustinian rule. The stricter discipline and greater emphasis on community life and devotion was in strong contrast to the happy-go-lucky sort of monasticism dear to the Celtic mind. But it is significant that the newer monasticism never made the same appeal to Cornishmen. Throughout the medieval period the monastic houses were largely dependent and mostly small. They were recruited to a great extent from outside the county.

An amusing incident recorded of the inhabitants of Bodmin and the priory there in 1113 throws a light upon conditions and beliefs common in the town. In that year some canons of Laon in France were on a begging tour with some relics of Our Lady, allegedly miraculous and highly profitable in consequence. In the course of their journey they came west, and were entertained by prior Algar at Bodmin. The relics were displayed. A blind girl, Kenehellis, was cured by touching the sacred objects. In the excitement that followed, the relative merits of rival spiritual powers being no doubt canvassed, a dispute began about King Arthur; it was stoutly maintained by a Cornishman in conversation with a foreigner that he was still alive, and would return. This the Frenchman ridiculed. An uproar broke out and the prior was hard put to it to prevent the angered crowd outside from sweeping into the church to eject the visitors. After this there were no more miracles. Obviously Celtic loyalties, centred on Arthur as the hero-figure, were very much alive in 1113.

To the Normans is attributed the inception of the practice of appropriation of livings. Some local lord as builder of the church on his estate, originally gave land and tithe of the estate produce for the support of the priest whom he would naturally appoint. It may have been the uncertain conditions attaching to patronage by the lord of the manor, or desire to augment the income or influence of monastic foundations or cathedral chapters, that the practice began of granting or obtaining the right of presentation and the right to the tithes for the monastery or chapter, making the condition that the pastoral duties in the parish should be cared for by a priest placed in the stead of the rector, as his 'vicarius'. Hence began the familiar, and to many puzzling, duality of titles for parish priests. As early as 1186 bishop John Fitzduke bestowed the benefice of St. Issey on the cathedral chapter. Perranuthnoe was granted for repairs of the cathedral. A charge on St. Just-in-Roseland provided incense for festivals at the cathedral. Gwennap, St. Winnow, Sancreed and Trevalga were appropriated to the cathedral chapter early in the thirteenth century, and so on.

Appropriation was a serious grievance as it diverted money from individuals and was a drain on the Church in Cornwall as a whole. The vicarial substitutes were often poorly paid, and many instances of intervention by the bishop, or appeals to the bishop for juster terms, are recorded for this period. The bishops favoured the practice as it removed patronage of the parishes from lay hands into ecclesiastical and monastic ones. By the close of the Middle Ages out of 212 parishes in Cornwall 125 were appropriated, and more than a quarter of the benefice income went out of the county. Attempts to limit the abuse were made, on the grounds that the larger communities and the chapters rapidly accumulated wealth. The Statute of Mortmain enacted in 1279 made royal assent necessary for new grants to Church corporations. Pope Boniface VIII issued in 1296 the Bull *Clericus Laicus* forbidding the clergy to give aid to secular authorities from Church funds, and in obedience to this Convocation withheld a subsidy demanded by the king. In consequence there were reprisals against the clergy, and thirty of the Cornish clerics were imprisoned in the gaol at Launceston. The pope withdrew the Bull, but a fillip had been given to anti-papal feelings.

The religious order of Friars Preachers was founded at Toulouse in 1215 by St. Dominic, and the Friars Minor, or Franciscans, by St. Francis in 1210. Both orders grew rapidly, and spread widely.

The Dominicans arrived in England in 1221, the Franciscans in 1224. The former were learned men, dedicated to the preservation of the faith by study and argument. The latter chose to minister to the outcasts of society.

The Franciscans established a house at Bodmin, but the exact date of its beginning is not known. It is said the founder was one John of London, a merchant, and that the resources of the friary were augmented by gifts from Earl Richard of Cornwall in 1239. The church was apparently in existence by 1253, since in that year Robert Clapthoyr, a thief, sought sanctuary there and in the friary abjured the kingdom. Many leading Cornishmen were buried in the church (which was a large one, standing on the site of the present Assize Court) including members of the Peverell and Carmynow families. The list of obits or memorial days for departed founders included the names of many illustrious persons.

The Dominican house at Truro has an even more shadowy history. It lay in the west of the present town, and owned considerable property in the Kenwyn valley, including a farm at Carvedras. In 1354 building operations of some kind were going on, and the Black Prince gave them oaks for the woodwork. The church, however, was in being in 1259, as bishop Bronescombe consecrated it on 29th September in that year. Not a trace of it remains today, though the seal turned up in a garden in Kent!

In Cornwall the two friaries attracted a good deal of support, and many benefactions – mostly small, however – continued to be made to them right up to the Dissolution in 1538. The number of friars seems to have been but a handful when compared with the houses in other counties.

The ministry of the wandering friar, popular with the people at first, was resented both by the members of the older religious orders and by the parish clergy. The advent of the friar unsettled the parochial routine, the homely discourses with topical illustrations weaned away those who should have attended the parish services, and the granting of easy absolution by the friar-priests tended to rouse prejudice against the clergy. And the begging friar drew off funds which – in the opinion of the clergy – should have gone to the parish churches.

A reflection of the new climate of thought prevailing in the middle thirteenth century is seen in the great amount of church building which dates from the period.

In the high summer of 1259 no less than nineteen Cornish parishes were making preparations for the dedication of their parish churches. Some of these were in every way new, some were rebuilt on ancient sites hallowed by Celtic piety, some had been reconstructed from Norman beginnings.

Many churches erected by the Normans had become in time either ruinous or too small for the increased population. The style now prevailing was in contrast to that rather grim and dark architecture. The windows were graceful lancets, the arches brought to a point, with slender pillars supporting them. Towers, sometimes with a spire, were often added at the west end.

When the harvest was in and travelling in the far west possible with some comfort the bishop who was to dedicate these churches came to Cornwall. His journey was greatly facilitated by his widespread episcopal manors, which formed convenient lodging places. It was a Devon man, Walter de Bronescombe, who occupied the Exeter see at the time, having been enthroned the year before. From 24th September 1259, to 25th October of the same year Bronescombe dedicated nineteen parish churches in Cornwall, and the church of the Friars Preachers (Dominicans) at Truro.

The buildings he dedicated have, of course, been further reconstructed or altered in later building enthusiasms, and the Dominican church at Truro is no more. But the little church at St. Anthony-in-Roseland (though heavily and badly restored) is much in the same shape and condition as Bronescombe saw it. It is cruciform, with a central tower with spire. Other remains of thirteenth century work in the Bronescombe churches can be seen at Sheviock, the tower at Looe, and smaller traces elsewhere.

The occasion of a rededication was often used to replace the old Celtic saint name by that of a saint more widely known. Sometimes the process of time may have assimilated the old name to one sounding like it. But an increasing tendency to abandon the Celtic dedications can be traced. St. Piala of Phillack becomes St. Felicitas; Meriadoc of Camborne becomes St. Martin, St. Dominica becomes St. Dominic, St. Anietus (or similarly-named Celtic pioneer), St. Neot. The unknown St. Veep survives only as a place name, the church in 1336 being dedicated to St. Cyriacus and Julitta. It is not without interest that two new churches dedicated by Bronescombe on his 1259 itinerary – Truro and Looe – were dedicated to St. Mary, reflecting at once the greater emphasis on the place of the Virgin in devotion and theology, and the outmoding of the ancient saints of the land.

Bishop Bronescombe – Walter le Goode – was the first of the bishops of Exeter to keep a register of his official acts. He was, of course, like most medieval bishops, constantly required to act in matters of State importance. He was prominent in the commission charged to work out a settlement after the battle of Evesham and the defeat of Simon de Montfort's faction. He attended the fourteenth General Council of the Church in Lyons in 1274, which achieved a temporary but formal union between the Latin and Greek Churches.

Some enlargements of churches had been called for as a result of the cult of reverence of relics. The veneration of personal trophies of dead heroes and martyrs goes back a long way in Christian history, but it was at its height in medieval times. There was a busy trade in these things, and the popular demand for them inevitably led to a spate of spurious objects being provided to excite the wonder – and the gifts – of the faithful.

The people of Perranzabuloe had as their proud possession – with some likelihood of their being genuine – the head of St. Piran, a cross and copper bell which once belonged to him, a pastoral staff, and the bier on which his body was carried. They also had relics of other saints. This was in 1281. Fifty years later a Commission of the Dean and Chapter reported that these relics had been ceremonially carried 'in an unwarrantable manner in various and even distant places'.

St. Piran of Perranzabuloe was a well-attended place of pilgrimage right up to the Reformation. A gift of relics of St. Germanus of Auxerre, who is supposed to have come to the west to extirpate the Pelagian heresy among Cornish Christians, led to the enlargement of the south aisle of the great church of St. Germans so as to accommodate the crowds who gathered at the shrine.

The relics of St. Petroc were, of course, kept at Bodmin. In 1177 one of the canons there had been placed under discipline for some misdemeanour, and in revenge had absconded, carrying the relics with him. He found refuge in the Breton monastery of St. Meen, whose brethren were not ashamed – but on the contrary delighted – to have such a rich addition to their store of relics. The canons of St. Petroc, however, appalled by the loss to their devotions, and their funds, appealed to King Henry II to press for their return. This was done, and the sacred objects came back to Cornwall in a beautiful casket of ivory plates. It is a quirk of history that the relics are lost, the casket remains. One of the finest treasures of its kind, it can be seen today, itself a relic, enshrined in the wall of Bodmin parish church.

We should be less surprised that devotion should outrun integrity and sound theology when we consider how elementary was the education of the clergy. Many would be but half-instructed, with only a smattering of theology and the most sketchy knowledge of Scripture. They were largely recruited from the peasant class. A promising youngster or a poor student might begin as holy water boy, and accompany the parish priest in his duties, learning by rote the Latin words of the offices and the simple music of the chants. In due course he might be advanced to one of the minor orders.

With little sense of dedication, benefices were too often looked upon as means of livelihood and advantage. Pluralities were frequent. Many pluralists accumulated three or more livings and served them by poorly paid curates. Absenteeism was another abuse, many clergy finding Cornwall less agreeable as a place of residence than elsewhere and leaving in their stead a deacon or curate. The great family of the Arundells of Lanherne were patrons of the rich benefice of St. Columb, which they filled with priests who seldom resided in Cornwall though they drew the revenues of the benefice. There were, of course in this great church many other priests serving chantries and parochial chapels.

Nor should the misdeeds and abuses, which naturally in every generation find mention in court records and other documents, make us forget there were in all probability not a few parish priests who served their people without thought of advance according to their knowledge and skill. Chaucer's *Poor Parson* may be an idealization, but that there were many who came near to achieving that ideal, we may not doubt.

Attempts were made from time to time to improve the low state of education of the clergy. Sometimes leave of absence was given for the purpose of study at Oxford or Cambridge, or abroad. There were of course no seminaries or theological colleges. In 1287 bishop Quivil ordered his clergy to obtain and to read a primer of Church doctrine, and in 1314 bishop Stapeldon founded at Oxford the Hall which bore his name, later known as Exeter College, and a famous nursery of many a West country cleric.

Intended to become a powerful influence in the Cornish Church Glasney College, dedicated to St. Mary and St. Thomas of Canterbury, was founded by bishop Bronescombe in 1264 in the valley behind Penryn. It was a college of secular canons in priests' orders. They were to be present at all services in their own church, were ruled by a provost, and possessed statutes based upon those of the cathedral chapter. The work of the college was to be seen in worship, learning and teaching. But the establishment never quite lived up to its intention. The conduct of members of the community left much to be desired, and in time, in spite of repeated commissions and inquiries, there were reports – well founded it seems – of the canons harbouring women, neglecting the services, and allowing property to be missing. The College, of course, suffered in the suppression of chantries in the sixteenth century, though as it was a secular community efforts were made to save it as a school or a fortress. Today hardly a vestige remains, though within its walls was written the cycle of plays in Cornish still treasured and which testify to the place in Cornish culture Glasney might have had.

Glasney was a new foundation. Some important Celtic centres continued as collegiate churches, with a handful of prebends or canons associated in common worship and the local cure of souls. Such places as St. Teath, Crantock, Probus, St. Endellion, St. Buryan are the best known and in a much attenuated form the two latter survived the changes of the sixteenth and seventeenth centuries, St. Buryan retaining its dean until 1864 and St. Endellion – uniquely in the county still retaining its college of prebendaries. St. Michael Penkevil was founded as a college in 1320 with an archpriest and three brethren, but it lapsed, and by 1426 the parish was an ordinary rectory.

The political course of events but seldom in this age

impinged directly on the inhabitants of the remoter parts of Cornwall.

But in the summer of 1348, with the news of the battle of Crècy, arrived an enemy whose depredations were felt from one end of the country to the other. The Black Death, probably the bubonic plague, was first detected in Dorset and spread with terrible rapidity. Devon and Cornwall were soon affected and many hundreds died in the year 1348–49. Seaports, with infection reinforced with every incoming trader, and towns such as Bodmin, where insanitary hovels huddled without air and proper water supply, were forcing grounds for the disease. A figure of 20,000 dead in Cornwall alone is seriously set forth by some authorities. At Bodmin priory the prior and all but two canons died. The prior of Minster, the prior of St. Michael's Mount, the dean of Crantock and many parochial clergy were early victims. Throughout the county livings became vacant, and it has been estimated that the death rate among the clergy that year was eight times the average.

The full effect of this plague was seen only over a distance of time. There was the enhancing of prices through the scarcity of labour, altered conditions in agriculture, a pause in development of the nation, a breakdown in craftsmanship, and a slackening of administration. Men began to call in question a Church which, claiming so much in the way of obedience and loyalty, seemed in spite of its prayers and processions to be powerless to halt the march of the ravaging disease. Of course this awakening doubt would be offset by the faithful care for parishioners exercised, we may not doubt, by many among the parochial clergy.

In Cornwall the accumulation of troubles which drove the peasants into revolt elsewhere did not bear so hardly. Nevertheless there was a lowered respect towards the clergy and the Church, and an increase in violence. In 1357 the priest of Poundstock, Penfound, was just finishing mass when an angry crowd of parishioners entered and slew him in the chancel. In St. Hilary parish in 1380 John Browder, a soldier in the king's service, seized Walter Sancre, a priest, and cut off his head. In 1382 the officiating priest and others were assaulted in the church at Crantock, and the following year a priest was dragged through the narrow streets of Penryn, Church property was stolen, and there is an accumulation of evidence that Church and clergy were subject to an increasing criticism and dislike.

These were the days of John Wycliffe and the Lollards, and though there does not seem to be much evidence of direct contact, the ideas of these independent thinkers nevertheless penetrated the county. Laurence Bedeman, a fellow of Exeter, wearing his vestments, but 'entering the fold to ravage the sheep' came into Cornwall in 1372 on a preaching tour. Later he made his peace with the Church and died as rector of Lifton in Devon. No doubt his views found ready ears, as some in the county had already ventured their own ideas in the growing spirit of inquiry and independent thought. In 1354 Ralph de Tremur, a former rector of Warleggan, a windy parish on the Bodmin moor, was accused of having denied the Real Presence and had burnt the consecrated host. He had become notorious for his heretical opinions and as he could converse fluently in Latin, French, English and Cornish he was able to disseminate his views widely.

The general unrest and adventuring of ideas inimical to the settled state of the Church led, not to the placing of emphasis on clear simple teaching but on repression. In 1400 the papal Bull *De Haeretico Comburendo* was set forth in a desperate attempt to hold back the advance of ideas by the terrible threat of being burnt alive by the State at the request of the Church on conviction of obstinate heresy.

The papacy itself had not been giving the witness of responsible care for the Church, since the rival popes, and the schism in Catholicism which resulted, weakened the dominance of the papacy over men's minds, while new discoveries and broader vision had come with travel and pilgrimage.

There was much nonetheless which outwardly promised the continuance of things as they were. In Cornish parishes in the fifteenth century a new wave of devotion began to make itself felt. After the close of the Hundred Years' War it was possible again to make pilgrimage to popular shrines overseas, such as St. James of Compostela. Local shrines abounded, the most popular being the Mount, St. Piran's, the Holy Trinity at St. Day, and others which grew in prosperity.

Rebuildings and additions to many parish churches were going on. Nearly every Cornish church was added to in this century, producing the edifices we know today. The builders were by this time able to use granite freely, and raised their arcades often in monoliths, with carved bases and capitals. The typical church of this period has three aisles, the Norman or later transepts having been swept away or drastically modified. Towers in the north of the county are tall and stately with a band of carved ornament near the foot, while in the west they are often squat and built without buttresses. Beautiful additions were made in the furnishings. Many Cornish churches display stoups for holy water, shrines, altarpieces and so forth in the comely Cataclewse stone, deriving perhaps from a workshop near St. Merryn. St. Ives church, though then not parochial, was finished and consecrated in 1428 as a brave venture by the townsfolk who desired to have full parochial rights but were frustrated by the mother parish of Lelant. St. Columb Major tower was being built in 1433, and seven years later the tower at Morval. The activity continued in fact right through the century to the very threshold of the Reformation. St. Mary, Launceston's beautiful fabric was commenced in 1511 and consecrated in 1524. Bodmin parish church, the largest in the county, was rebuilding

1469–91 and the accounts for its building and furnishing still survive.

In the fifteenth and sixteenth centuries the walls of the church would be covered with frescoes or painted pictures of saints and symbols, such as may be traced still at Breage, Linkinhorne, Poughill and elsewhere. The windows were a blaze of colour, with the story of the local saint (as still at St. Neot), Biblical pictures, or ecclesiastical figures, as at St. Winnow. On the screens dividing the nave – which was used for secular purposes – from the chancel the carver and painter exercised his greatest art. The West country preserves examples of chancel screens of an interesting variety of styles. The best in Cornwall are those at St. Buryan, St. Winnow, St. Ewe, St. Mawgan and Lanreath, but these have been restored, and the lofts, destroyed in the Reform iconoclasm, replaced. A modern screen which gives a good idea of the medieval coloured screen may be seen at Blisland.

In earlier medieval days the congregation would stand or kneel on the sanded or rush-strewn floor, with recourse, if elderly, to a stone bench against the wall or round a pillar. Later there came the wooden pews, with carved ends in heraldic or symbolic patterns. Some churches, as Mullion, preserve the whole range of complete seats; many others have a wealth of carved ends, the seats themselves having been replaced.

In the chancels and chapels the altars, richly furnished, were appropriated to the use of various gilds, or for masses for the parochial or noble dead. The high altar, of course, stood at the east wall of the chancel, and would be arrayed in the changing colours for the church season. In Cornish churches no doubt the use of Exeter was followed if the appointments were full. But in many parish churches there were surprising gaps, if we may judge by the presentments, or complaints made to the archdeacon's court, from time to time. Dilapidated books, vestments in insufficient number or condition, lack of linen for the altars, no pyx for the reserved sacrament, lack of a censer for incense, and so on were often reported. Indeed, it appears that only a small proportion of churches possessed censers, and incense must have been unused in all but about a quarter of the parish churches at this period.

Latin of course was used for the service, which followed the local missal with the permitted diocesan variations. The holy water clerk would assist the priest to vest, taking his vestments from the altar or from a chest near it. He would go with the priest for the sprinkling of the people before mass. At the Elevation, an emphasized point in the late medieval service, the people would look up to see the raised host and chalice and the bell would sound from the tower. Music from a few singers might grace the service, and here and there in larger churches a simple organ might help the singing. There was such an instrument at Launceston in 1461, and in 1538 at Bodmin Friary and St. Michael's Mount.

The greater part of the populace would be present at mass on Sundays and many would remain for later services such as vespers. Weekday masses attracted a smaller number and might at times have been a duet between priest and clerk. Some remote chapelries might have only an occasional mass.

The local gentry and lord of the manor, and later on even the more well-to-do merchants, aped the nobility in pressing for private chapels in their own houses, in which their own chaplain might officiate at mass; they were a kind of status symbol, in fact. An early example of a Cornish domestic chapel of this kind was at Bosworgey in St. Erth, to which a licence was issued for the celebration of mass about 1260. In granting such licence a promise was usually exacted that the parish church should not be prejudiced, and in this particular case the applicant, Sir William de Roscrou, was required to pay all offerings to the parish wardens, and to give as a token of subjection 1 lb. of wax to the high altar of the parish church of St. Erchus annually.

By the end of the medieval period even the smaller landowners and richer merchants aspired to have their domestic chapels. Sometimes a nearby Celtic site or shrine might be rescued, as perhaps at Halton in St. Dominic.

Apart from the parish churches and domestic chapels, the countryside would feature occasionally a chapel of the local hermit. A hermitage was not an enclosed cell, but, if the description may be allowed, was similar to a one-man monastery in that the hermit, who had to be duly authorized by the bishop, had a legitimate territory in which he was free to roam and work. Some hermits in Cornwall apparently tended lights on the hills or coasts to guide travellers. There were hermits at Castle Park, Liskeard; near the castle at Restormel; Roche Rock, and perhaps at St. Michael's Mount, Hellesbury Beacon, and the chapel on Rough Tor.

Serving a different purpose were the chantry chapels associated with the parish church. These provided convenience for the offering of mass for the distinguished dead – some local noble, or generous benefactor. Many craft guilds served as primitive welfare clubs, and included masses and prayers for their deceased members. Priests to serve the chantries would be provided with some small endowment, coupled perhaps with the oversight of a few scholars, to celebrate mass daily for the souls of the faithful. The relations between the parish priest and the chantry priests of his own church were not seldom the cause of friction and strife.

Often the chantry altar was simply one of those in the church itself. Occasionally a separate building might be provided, as at Bodmin where the roofless ruin of St. Thomas chapel is supposed to have been such a chantry. At St. Austell and at St. Kew the original chantries are thought to have been just outside the walls of the parish church and to have been incorporated within the main building when it was enlarged. Many such chantries existed in the parishes of Cornwall, and the chantry property was in total a considerable amount.

At the threshold of reform the monastic communities in Cornwall included but small numbers. In 1492 there were at Launceston priory only ten brethren, and at Bodmin probably the same number. St. Germans and Tywardreath numbered only seven, Truro Dominican friary had eleven, and the Franciscans at Bodmin eight. There were no nunneries in Cornwall. The property owned by these small houses was extensive, and its administration left much to be desired.

Perhaps the real fault was not so much corruption – there is little evidence of real wickedness among the brethren – as that the monasteries and friaries had run down and ceased to serve the purpose for which they were founded. In some cases the monastic house held the lordship of a local town, as at Fowey, which in the vigorous sixteenth century and with the new importance of the sea irked at its subjection to the priory at Tywardreath. With some reason, for the prior there was a bibulous waster and the whole place notoriously slack. The emerging families, aware of the new direction of things, were envious of the monastic possessions and the grip of the ancient houses. Criticism of the moral leadership of the papacy and the clergy, growing belief that many church practices were 'superstitious', the abuses of the ecclesiastical courts which touched life at so many points, all pointed to the need for reform.

The medieval age moved on to the threshold of upheaval. The time was arriving for a fresh weighing of the traditional religion, and the distinguishing between the lawful developments from primitive Christianity and the mere abuses springing from men's ambition and greed. Nevertheless Cornwall was not foremost in its questioning.

A conservative and backward-looking community such as it was would not welcome change.

And at this time there seemed to be much auguring the continuance of the old ways in spite of all. The great Arundells, the leading family of Cornwall, lived in state in their ancient manor house at Lanherne, now a nunnery. The last prior but one of Bodmin, Thomas Vyvyan, a Cornishman, was consecrated titular bishop of Megara in 1517 in order to act as suffragan to bishop Oldham of Exeter. With him at Bodmin, it was as if Cornwall once again had its own bishop. He maintained, on a grand scale, the princely rule of a prelate of the old order. Much preferment came his way, and at Rialton, the chief manor of the Bodmin monastery, he had built a charming house, about 1510, a notable portion of which still remains. At his death an elaborate tomb was erected over his bones, which from motives uncommon in the Reformation upheavals was transferred to the parish church where it may still be seen.

Bishop John Veysey held the see of Exeter for more than thirty years, having been consecrated two years after Vyvyan, till his death in 1554, with only a short intermission when he gave way to the reformer Miles Coverdale. Though a consecrator of Cranmer, he was a man of the old ways, a courtier, a prelate of the cast common in Renaissance days. In Cornish parishes the clergy included men of ability such as Dr. John Moreman, vicar of Menheniot, 1529–54. He wrote a commentary on the epistle to the Romans – a favourite epistle for reformers – aided as scribe (like many later clergy he was a notoriously bad writer) by Lawrence Travers, vicar of Quethiock. A man beloved of the people for his championing of the old religion, he was the first to teach his people the Lord's prayer, creed, and commandments in English.

This recognition of the English tongue in east Cornwall is a reminder that apart from the miracle plays there was no large body of literature in the native tongue by which it might resist the growth of English usage. Had there been a corpus of Cornish literary works, the ancient speech may well have survived, as Welsh has done. However, the miracle plays stand as evidence of what might have been. They helped to keep alive homely devotion, and tended to delay the extinction of Cornish as a spoken language.

Written about 1509 *Beunans Meriasek,* the life of the patron saint of Camborne, is the one surviving example of the sort of thing once possessed by every parish. At feast-tide the clergy got their people together in the local 'Playing Place' to enact in primitive fashion the story of their patron saint, with generous legendary and elevating additions.

Covering a wider scope than the miracle plays are the three long plays collectively known as the *Ordinalia* – the subjects being the Origin of the World, the Passion of Our Lord, and his Resurrection.

These three more ambitious plays emanated probably from Glasney college, and with a moving sincerity they combine moments of bucolic comedy and buffoonery.

The inhabitants of Cornwall at the close of the fifteenth century needed distraction and the drawing of their thoughts to eternal things, since there were harsh conditions in this life to bear. Another levy to finance war with the Scots lay heavy on the county, and in 1497 the collectors found growing resistance to their demands. At St. Keverne the blacksmith, Michael Joseph, assumed leadership of the people in opposing the levy, and a Bodmin lawyer, Flamank, fanned the will to revolt with his eloquence.

Throughout the summer of 1497 an increasing rabble of half-armed Cornishmen marched through Devon and Somerset, to reach eventually the environs of London. Here the rebels prepared to give battle to the forces of the king, Henry VII. They pitched their field at Blackheath, and in the action which followed the rebels were surrounded by the royal forces, cut to pieces, and their leaders taken and in due course executed. Only a couple of months after the suppression of this revolt Perkin Warbeck landed at Land's End and made his way to Bodmin, where he was proclaimed as Richard IV. The late discontents were unappeased, and a force of some three thousand flocked to join him.

The story, however, was repeated – the army pressed on to Exeter and Taunton, Warbeck fled before the fresh reinforcements of the king, and the leaderless Cornish in their anger happened on the luckless provost of Glasney, who had been an assiduous collector of the taxes which had caused the first rebellion earlier in the year. In the marketplace of Taunton he was barbarously cut to pieces.

Henry sent commissioners into Cornwall to settle the county, and laid a fine of £623 on the people. The raising of the sum allotted to each district was often the responsibility of the unfortunate parson. It seemed as if the Church hierarchy was indifferent to the plight of the common people, and appeared to be too closely identified with the authority exacting the hated taxes. And the almost-success of these rebellions in due course encouraged yet another, which as we shall see, had as a principal cause the religious changes imposed on the nation in the following reigns.

3

Reformation and Commonwealth

THE REIGN OF HENRY VIII, SO MOMENTOUS FOR THE CHURCH, so vitalizing to the nation, began in 1509. Within two years the country was at war again with France. As would increasingly be the case in the future, Cornwall was drawn into the struggle, particularly taking its share in war at sea. Leading families of the county had fathers or sons in the retinue of Henry as he travelled on the Continent, and in the new-found naval force Cornishmen would largely figure.

At home the effects of war bore hardly. Levy of men, taxation growing in weight, riots among the tinners, and in 1513 threat of invasion lay heavy on the community. But nothing of this detracted from the king's own popularity; he stood as it were a symbol of the growing awareness of itself of the nation.

Peace in 1525 saw the Cornish churches in a surge of rebuilding and enrichment. The churchwardens of Stratton were ordering a new screen from John Daw and John Pares in 1531. Other screens at St. Ewe, St. Buryan, St. Winnow and Lanreath were being constructed, and bench ends in great numbers date from this time. The windows at St. Neot, with their scenes from the life of the saint, were put in during the 1530s, while the tower at St. Austell, the churches at Truro and Launceston were all abuilding. At

Probus the parishioners, led by John Tregian of Golden, were lending their carts to draw the stone for the magnificent tower there, which was hardly completed before the first gusts of the Reformation storm began to blow.

The air was full of strange rumours of anti-papal views and struggles on the Continent. Henry's reign had opened on a note of orthodoxy. He had entered the lists against Luther's teaching – which he disliked till the end of his life – with a defence of the traditional seven sacraments. This work, for Henry was no mean scholar, earned him a papal commendation and the title 'Defender of the Faith' from Leo X in 1521. In joy over this, bishop Veysey erected in his chapel the Royal Arms.

The sunshine of papal and orthodox favour, however, was not to last long. Henry prepared for his struggle with the pope over the marriage question, and the 'king's matter' became an affair touching national pride and independence. The Parliament of 1529 was eager to support him – some say it was packed carefully by the king – and it reflected the nationalistic and forward-looking views of the up-and-coming families. As a result of the pope's inability to give Henry his desire, the Act of Supremacy finally brought to an end the ecclesiastical jurisdiction of the pope in this country. The Crown was made the source of jurisdiction in Church matters, but not of course its spiritual authority. The pope replied by excommunicating Henry.

The Reformation, so disastrous, so splendid, was fairly launched. The 'king's matter' was but the immediate cause. The whole is the unfolding of a tangle of social, economic, national factors as well as of ones theological and ecclesiastical.

The enormous cost of Henry's war and the huge expenses of his court had impoverished the country, and he turned covetous eyes towards the monasteries and their accumulated wealth. Their dissolution was decided upon, and in 1535 a general visitation of universities and monastic foundations was announced. Partly conviction as to their uselessness as spiritual centres, partly sheer avarice, and partly resentment at their galling property rights underlay this move, with the additional and comforting thought that they were a sphere of lingering papal sympathy.

Henry in his self-conferred position as Supreme Head exercised his powers of visitation through Thomas Cromwell, whom he appointed Vicar-general, an office hitherto, and since, unknown in history. In the west Cromwell was assisted by Dr. John Tregonwell, a lawyer and a Cornishman, of Catholic, conservative sympathies who was not above turning the new moves to his own advantage. There were not a few like him.

The Cornish religious houses were not large in comparison with those elsewhere. Three houses only, Launceston, St. Germans and Bodmin, had an annual income of over £200 and so escaped the Act of 1536 suppressing the smaller monasteries. Tywardreath was the first to go; its income was only £123. Its prior, Collins, had succeeded in 1506, and in the years that followed its decay was notorious. Unfavourable accounts were given to Veysey in 1521 and it seems that Collins often succumbed to drink and allowed the rule at the priory to lapse. Naturally the priory rights over Fowey were resented, particularly by the Treffrys of that town, tenants to the priory. Prior Collins managed to provide for his relations before he was replaced just before the Dissolution, making out a lease of priory lands to his cousin.

The friaries fell in 1538, the process of suppression having been held up for a time by the Pilgrimage of Grace and the northern Rising, which had no counterpart in the west. The greater monasteries of Bodmin, St. Germans and Launceston were dissolved in 1539. Compensation was paid to the dispossessed monks. Prior Shere of Launceston had a pension of £100 a year; prior Swymmer of St. Germans and prior Wandsworth (or Mundy) of Bodmin each received £66 13s. 4d., their monks were offered either a pension of some £6 a year, or the presentation to a parish. The monastic buildings were plundered and used as quarries for generations.

The slow process of the Dissolution had given time for the more astute heads of monastic houses to make provision, and to deal out property among their relations and friends. Wandsworth, whose election to Bodmin after the death of Vyvyan had been helped by his steward Nicholas Prideaux, provided for his own future in such a way. The two families were linked by marriage. The Padstow property of the monks passed into the ownership of the Prideaux line. The priory buildings at Bodmin were leased by the Crown to Thomas Sternhold, whose mark on Church history is in the versification of the psalms made by him and long used in the protestant services.

Elsewhere followed on the same lines the sale or lease of monastic lands to wealthy merchants or lesser gentry. On such a basis many Cornish families began their course as landowners – Carews, Treffrys, Rashleighs, Prideaux, Eliots. They adapted the old monastic buildings as residences, enlarged their old houses or built new. From its inception the Reformation was a social upheaval using, and used by, the new theological opinions; it cannot be understood merely from an ecclesiastical viewpoint.

Meanwhile changes in teaching, ritual, and the modes of worship were being considered. There were to be no more pilgrimages, relics were to be taken away and so forth. Henry's last blow against the old order was the suppression of the chantries and the issue in 1546 of a commission for the making of a survey of all chantries, colleges, gilds, hospitals and free chapels and their property. At this point Henry died (leaving, ironically, in his will a provision for daily masses at his tomb), and was succeeded by his sickly son Edward VI, in the care of his uncle Somerset till his coming-of-age.

The new government began in 1548 with the further implementing of Henry's last blow. New commissions were set up by the Privy Council in each county to take an inventory of the chantry goods and arrange for their sale. The commissioners for Cornwall were William Godolphin, Henry Chiverton, and John Grenville. Through all the winter of 1548 they were at work in the county. Here and there an endowment was spared or transferred, where there was an educational provision, as at Week St. Mary, where Dame Perceval's school was allowed to transfer to Launceston, but the great majority of chantry and college goods were confiscated with all their plate and furnishing into royal ownership. The commission seems to have had some desire to save Glasney college either as a school or as a fortified place to defend the coast, but in vain. The buildings were sold, in time crumbled away, and today scarcely a stone of Bronescombe's foundation remains.

In 1548 orders were issued that changes were to be made in the services in the parish churches – candles were to be no more blessed on Candlemas Day, nor ashes on Ash Wednesday or palms on Palm Sunday. Images superstitiously used were to be removed.

Now though there had been momentous alterations made by Henry in the government of the Church these were little more than matters of academical discussion to the populace. Payments once made to Rome were to be made still – to the king. But the suppression of the monasteries, with the consequent throwing on the market of many who had worked there, craftsmen who had erected and repaired buildings, and the cessation of the relief given to the poor, was another matter. And now with the meddling in every parish service in the land every parishioner was affected by the new trend in religion.

The standard of revolt was speedily raised against the advisors and Council of the young king. The parish of St. Keverne was in the fore again, as in the previous half century. William Body, a layman, who had leased the archdeaconry of Cornwall from an illegitimate son of Cardinal Wolsey – a world of medieval abuses speaks in that transaction – was destroying the statues in Helston church in pursuance of the order. A mob of over a thousand assembled, led by Martin Geoffrey, a priest of St. Keverne, and William and John Kilter of Constantine. Body was dragged out of the house where he had taken refuge, and stabbed to death. This revolt was crushed with the help of the gentry from the eastern part of the county. The expenses of meat, drink and horses for the men opposing the rebels were sometimes paid for by the parishes. At St. Nighton's in St. Winnow a bell and a chalice were sold to raise funds for this purpose, and there were similar payments at Stratton and Launceston.

This incident was but a prelude to more serious trouble. In 1549 Parliament enforced the use of an English liturgy – the Book of Common Prayer, to replace the Latin liturgy and the varied diocesan uses. This simplified book retained the old mass vestments, with much of the old theology and liturgical use, translated into English by Cranmer. It was, however, new, and much mystery of worship was absent in its use. It was to be used for the first time on Whitsunday, which fell that year on 9th June. At Sampford Courtenay, a village on the border of Dartmoor, the congregation refused the new service (conservative as it seems to us now), forced the priest to say mass according to the old rite the following day and prepared to rise. The movement spread. Cornishmen had also demanded their mass, for many in the west could not understand the English even as much as the Latin, for the latter was at least familiar in its cadences.

The Cornish insurgents gathered at Bodmin, led by

the mayor, Henry Bray, John Winslade of Tregarrick and Humphry Arundell of Helland. A number of priests encouraged them, and no doubt had a hand in drawing up the articles of supplication to the king. The rebels objected to the changes in religion while the king was still a minor, and demanded the restoration of the old ways. The articles formulated by the rebels are given in several forms, mostly similar, but the final form was arrived at only after the juncture with the men of Devon.

Some of the west Cornwall gentry fled before the rebels and shut themselves in their houses. Meanwhile, rumours of the rising reached Lord Protector Somerset. He sent Sir Peter Carew and his brother Sir Gawen down to parley with the rebels. But, unhappily, no more unsuitable ambassadors could have been found. Were not the Carews representative of those who had everything to gain from a defeat of the rebels, men of the new order, who had profited from spoliation of monastic lands?

The rebels withdrew before the advance guard of the Carews, who thereupon had no one with whom to parley. The men of Cornwall having joined with the Devonshire force and gathered to themselves several gentlemen as supporters arrived before Exeter and began a siege – the second time in half a century that that city had been surrounded by Cornishmen. The rebels now formulated their final demands and forwarded them to the government. They wanted the old Latin service with its accustomed ritual and the restoration of the old devotions. They wanted Dr. Moreman and Dr. Crispin, who held their views, to be restored to them – they had been imprisoned – and preferred to some good benefices. They wanted the gentry to have but a limited number of servants and to restore half the monastic lands they had obtained. It is interesting, however, and significant, too, that they did not ask for the resumption of the Roman jurisdiction, but that things should be as during the last days of King Harry at least in the time of Edward's minority. They asked for Cardinal Pole, kinsman of the king, to be recalled and made a member of the Council. It was, in short, an English and national solution which the rebels asked for, though no doubt some inwardly hoped for the restoration of normal relations with Rome. These Articles were answered by Cranmer, now archbishop of Canterbury and Henry's tool in his marriage problems, and rejected.

At the beginning of July Lord Russell, 'President of the Council for the Western Parts', arrived before Honiton with an army and – so seriously did the government view the rising – with promised reinforcements of Italian and German mercenaries. In the weeks following the rebels were surrounded at Fenny Bridges, separated, and cut down. Cruel reprisals were meted out – the hanging of the leaders Winslade and Arundell, forfeiture of the estates of the guilty, execution of the priests, including the vicar of St. Veep and the vicar of Poundstock; the vicar of St. Thomas, Exeter, they hanged, clad in his vestments, from his tower top.

Russell left in Cornwall to settle the county Sir Anthony Kingston, whose ruthless and cynical proceedings have given him 'a name more memorable than commendable' amongst the Cornish.

With the crushing of active opposition, the process of governmental alterations in religion continued. A second Prayer book, still further removed from the medieval theology was introduced by Cranmer in 1552 as a result of the movement of his ideas towards developed protestantism. More ceremonies were abolished, only the surplice was allowed as a vestment, the stone altars were ordered to be replaced by wooden tables. At Poughill a table is shown, reputedly of this date. The precious metal ornaments in use in the churches, such as crosses, pyxes, censers and candlesticks, chalices and so forth were to be assessed by commissioners appointed for the purpose and confiscated to the crown. One chalice and one paten were allowed to remain in each parish. The bells had already all been ordered to be sold except for the smallest, to pay for the cost of reducing the rebels; in fact, only the clappers were taken.

In Cornwall the commission consisted of Sir Richard Edgcumbe, Thomas Treffry, Sir Hugh Trevanion, Sir William Godolphin, John Killigrew and John, first earl of Bedford. All these were new men, whose position and authority sprang from their acceptance of the new ideas and policies. From the lists of ornaments drawn up by the commission we can see the wealth of rich gifts made by benefactors and subscribed for by parishioners, especially in the case of larger churches.

Even in 1552, however, only a minority of parishes had crosses, censers and pyxes, though all had chalice and paten. The commission collected no less than 6,241 oz. of precious metal in the county, which was stored away in St. Mawes Castle to be transferred to London. That it was Church stuff, given by the people of the parishes, or ancient and beautiful in workmanship, mattered not a whit. The government needed money.

By this time the issues were clear and it was the parting of the ways. The recalcitrant faction centred mainly around the Arundells of Lanherne. In succeeding generations they were gradually squeezed out of public life along with other old families. The rise of the new men would be at the expense of their fall. But they were to enjoy a brief Indian summer before the winter of repression and deprivation. In 1553 the king died. Plans and policies fell to the ground, for the next occupant of the throne was the fervently Catholic Mary, who saw as her work the restoration of England to obedience to Rome.

The Prayer book enactments were repealed. Parliament ordered the resumption of the old rites, and the unfamiliar ceremonies, laid aside for years, were fumblingly carried out. The Cornish plate was recalled and redistributed, the stone altars re-erected, the vestments rediscovered (many had been taken for domestic ornaments). Parishes put up their figures on the roodscreens or, through poverty, or doubt as to the permanency of the reaction, erected painted canvas instead.

The year 1554 was spent in putting the diocese in some sort of order. Bishop Miles Coverdale, who had been intruded into the see over the head of the complaisant Veysey, was deprived, and the old bishop restored, for a brief tenure, terminated by his death. Clergy who had too daringly got themselves wives during the reign of Edward were firmly treated. They were offered the choice of being deprived, or if they put away their wives, could take another living in another part of the diocese. Only about eighteen Cornish clergy had married; prejudice was still strongly against the clergy having wives. William Lamb, rector of St. Keyne had taken a wife in the time of Edward. In Mary's time several J.P.s with a rabble invaded the rectory at midnight, seized the rector and his wife in bed and put them in the stocks at Duloe, where they sat for twelve hours!

Those made deacon or priest in the way of the new Edwardine Ordinal had their orders regularized, and everything possible was done to carry on as before Henry's intervention. Some things, of course, Mary could not do. She still unwillingly bore the title 'Supreme Head' till 1554, she had to appeal to Parliament for the introduction of the Latin use again, and she dare not restore the monastic lands and endowments of chantries, to which the new owners greedily clung.

When the persecutions – by which Mary's reign is popularly remembered – began, numbers of protestant valiants, clerical and lay, went abroad to the safe Reformed areas of Switzerland. Some went to Venice, Strasburg and Frankfurt. The complete freedom to express their protestant ideas did not lead to harmony; instead the Continent was scandalized by the factions and strife of the English refugees. But an impulse was given to Reformed ideas – the moderate men became zealots, the careless became convinced as they absorbed the ideas of Calvin and other continental giants.

Cornwall produced only one victim of Mary's burnings, a poor woman named Agnes Prest, of Northcote in the parish of Boyton. She had taken to heart the teaching she had heard in Edward's time, and made a nuisance of herself, thrusting herself into controversy when the authorities – who deemed her but a 'mazed creature' – would have taken no notice. The bishop, Turberville, asked her why she meddled in such matters as the sacrament of the altar which all the doctors of the world cannot define? She was set at liberty, but fell into an angry argument with a mason in the cathedral. At last she was taken again into prison, condemned and burnt at Southernhay, in Exeter, in 1558. The bishop's register is silent on this lamentable act.

Mary's betrothal to Philip of Spain aroused dismay and helped to crystallize anti-Catholic feeling in the growing fear of Spanish power and the ambition of its king. Meanwhile the Council of Trent, with sessions intermittently between 1545 and 1562 debated the questions raised by the Reformers, and set out to redefine the faith of the Roman Church in uncompromising terms and to prepare for the Counter Reformation. There were subtle differences in the continental Church before and after Trent. The most obvious was the replacement of various diocesan uses by the Roman Rite in 1570 and the enhanced place of the pope supported by the zeal of the Jesuits. Much medieval speculation was now codified or rejected.

Mary died in 1558, and Elizabeth came to the throne in a blaze of relief and hope. Her reign was to unfold, with a flourish, a magnificent canvas. Many who would otherwise have chosen to walk in the old ways had been alienated by Mary's bigotry, and in Elizabeth there was a flash of the old attractive gallantry of Henry. She was crowned with the old rites but slightly curtailed, and soon made her policy clear. The outlines of her father's hand were seen. The Latin mass was made illegal, the Second Book of Edward was restored to use, but with significant alterations in a Catholic direction. The old vestments of the 'second year of the reign of Edward VI' were to be retained and be in use. Denials of the Real Presence were removed. Commissioners toured each county to set the new order going, to receive the submission of the clergy and to see altars removed and images destroyed.

All Mary's bishops but one or two refused to accept the supremacy of Elizabeth – the title Supreme Governor replaced that of Supreme Head – and were deprived, being imprisoned or kept under surveillance. After the sacrifices they had exacted they could do no other than refuse the new oath. Many thought that papal supremacy offered the only hope of continuity, and opinion hardened on either side. Turberville, bishop of Exeter, was unable to take the oath acknowledging Elizabeth and renouncing the pope. He was safely lodged in the Tower for a short while. His place at Exeter was filled by William Alley, duly consecrated according to the English rite. Among the lower clergy there was little disturbance, and all but six – the parish priests of Creed, Menheniot, Altarnun, Lansallos, Lanteglos-by-Fowey, and St. Columb Major (he was bishop of St. Davids and non-resident) – took the oath, accepted the new order, and used the English Prayer book. The return made by Alley to archbishop Parker reveals that there were 104 unmarried and 17 married clergy in Cornwall, many pluralists, and about six were competent preachers.

Though only six had been deprived there was an acute shortage of clergy to staff the parishes, for the uncertainty of the previous years had stopped off the flow of ordination candidates. Alley set himself to remedy this lack, ordaining in Cornwall six deacons and two priests at Budock in 1565, and others at Egloshayle and Truro.

The first ten years of the reign of Elizabeth showed plainly her desire for inclusive tolerance. The bounds were widely set. Naturally in consequence there was diversity of use. Some parishes continued as many as they could of the ancient ceremonies, adapted to the English communion, and wore the vestments, after the mode of modern highchurchmen, of whom they were forerunners. At Bodmin John Dagle, an ex-monk, was no doubt instrumental in keeping (in use?) the ornaments noted in 1566 – cope, chasuble, tunicle, censer and other ornaments in connection with the communion. In the same year Stratton paid 2d. for 'mending off the vestments'. At Lostwithiel much later (1584) Henry Caesar the vicar wore a cope at the communion and read service in the old way. The local Puritans were irritated at his popularity; there was obviously much sympathy with his interpretation of the English religion. He ended his days as Dean of Ely.

In other parishes the vestments were sold, or given away or stolen for domestic use. The Menheniot vestments and plate were sold by auction at Liskeard in 1559. The mass books of Landulph and the rood figures there were burnt at Saltash in the same year. The influence of Calvinism was growing and was inimical to any uses suggesting the continuance of 'popery'.

The papacy itself did not speak on the matter of the Elizabethan legislation till 1570. Till then those who clung to the idea of papal supremacy continued to attend their parish churches, saddened no doubt by the signs of Reforming zeal which all too often was sheer wanton destruction. Possibly they received their communion privately from a Marian priest who said a secret mass, or the parish priest from such a service brought consecrated wafers for those of his people who desired them, using them in the English communion.

The greater proportion of those who were dissatisfied with the English middle way were those who wanted more sweeping reforms. At Mary's death the exiles from Zurich and Geneva and elsewhere returned, and their radical ideas, strongly Calvinistic and anti-ceremonial, were ceaselessly propagated, and, in eastern counties especially, accepted widely. Some few 'Puritans' were prepared to accept a modified episcopacy, but most favoured a presbyterian system as seeming to them the order plain in Scripture. Some were able, learned and conscientious pastors. Some were just fanatics, but all took exception to the liturgy as it stood and to certain ceremonies prescribed in the Prayer book, such as kneeling at communion, the ring in marriage, the sign of the cross in baptism, and so on. It became apparent as time went on that the system they wished to establish was irreconcilable with Anglicanism.

So far as Cornwall was concerned Puritanism was never the religion of more than a small minority of the people, but that minority was well-organized, well-informed, and to be reckoned with. The growth of Puritanism caused it to be a serious threat to the Anglican Church by the 1570s. The Prayer book order of service was evaded, or used with the hope that in time something more fully representing Reformed beliefs might be had. In such conditions it was unlikely that the use of the old vestments would continue, and indeed it became impossible to insist on more than the surplice in service-time.

Another event in 1570 moved the Church of England away still further to the Reformed position. The pope, Paul V, having long deliberated the matter, excommunicated Elizabeth and absolved her subjects from allegiance. This Bull, the *Regnans in Excelsis*, declared the queen to be heretic, illegitimate, excommunicate, and deposed. The only sufferers were her Roman Catholic subjects. There could be henceforth no toleration of those known to favour papal rule. Every Roman Catholic was suspect, and the championing by Philip of Spain of the cause of restoration of Romanism in England rendered them potential traitors, however innocent their devotion to Rome; it was not innocent in all. The struggle with the 'Recusants', those who held to Rome, must be studied in a separate chapter.

Symbolic of the trend towards more definitely Reformed ideas is the replacement of the old 'massing chalices'. In all Churches of the Reform it was a cardinal point that the laity should receive communion in both kinds. The use of the old vessels made this difficult in the case of the cup, which was designed for the use of the priest alone. Larger vessels were obviously necessary. Some parishes began to use domestic utensils. In 1576 or thereabouts – in eastern counties the date is a little before that and some few earlier examples survive in Cornwall too – an order was made to replace the mass chalices. Many Elizabethan cups made in obedience to the decree remain – about a hundred. Based on a tumbler-like model they yet include the traditional members of base, stem, knop and cup, and are beautifully proportioned with a cover-paten. John Johns of Exeter, John Yeds, and John Averie are the makers' names most frequently found.

The Puritan struggle, so integral to the story of English religion, reached its climax in the 1580s. By 1577 bishop Bradbridge was in trouble with a Puritan lecturer – a curate – at Liskeard, since his patron, Dr. Tremayne, was a great fancier of the men of that school. One of the most active Puritans was Eusebius Paget, an educated choirboy who became incumbent of Kilkhampton in 1580, in succession to John Grenville. The old man had gone along comfortably with all the changes under Henry and the following reigns and restored his church in the old style in the first years of Elizabeth. The new minister was a man of different stamp. In 1584 he was called before his bishop and deprived for not conforming to the Prayer book. His defence was, there was no such book at Kilkhampton to conform to, and counter-attacked his bishop for his nepotism. The Puritans drew up a survey of the state of the clergy, and their report is interesting as showing how well-informed they were, though biased as we might expect. Sixteen incumbents are marked as having 'popish tendencies' – that is, something corresponding to modern highchurchism. Nicholas Arscott of Cubert was a 'massman and a known papist'. The vicar of Lostwithiel was 'a notable papist and hath drawn his people to great idolatry'. The rector of Redruth was much suspected in that line and so on. A Supplication was prepared for the Parliament of 1586 pleading the Puritan point of view; they did not wish to secede from the Church, but to remodel it according to their own convictions.

We see at this point the beginnings of interaction and tension between parties in the Church of England. In 1606 certain ministers refused to subscribe the necessary oaths on presentation to benefices and the bishop, William Cotton, reasoned with them in vain; some of their number were suspended from office. Bishop Hall treated them a little more gently, in 1627 permitting Puritan lecturers to give additional sermons, and refraining from denouncing those of his clergy who in 1633 refused to read the Royal Declaration on the Book of Sports, which encouraged games after church on Sunday as in medieval days, to the great anger of the Puritan party. 'He used all fair and gentle means to win them to a good order', but for this he was delated before the king as a favourer of Puritanism.

The interplay of party struggle left many parishes in a state of confusion. Religious changes and the overthrow of many certainties once accepted broke the confidence of the rank and file. In spite of governmental pressure by way of fine for non-attendance at church, it is clear many were lost to any loyalty to religion. Bishop Cotton complained in

1600 that there were many atheists in his diocese, and many papists, especially near the Cornish coast, conventicles multiplied in fields and gardens, churches were profaned, and there was 'a slender observance' of Sabbath and holy days!

We need not, of course, suppose there were no diligent and devout parish clergy at this time. The Puritan condemnation of a large number merely means that these did not fulfil the strict requirements of that school. For instance, Carew, the writer of the delightful *Survey of Cornwall,* tells us admiringly of the parson of St. Ewe, Hugh Atwell. As physician, and reliever of want, he was justly famed. He prescribed milk, apples and fresh air as treatment for his patients, and was himself a testimony to his medicine, since he lived to be over ninety, a prodigious age for those days. Churches in the district benefitted by his generosity. Yet he is curtly dismissed in the Puritan comment 'he professeth physic'.

With the holding for the moment of the Puritan advance a new care for the appointments of worship and the parish churches may be discerned. It was the age of Nicholas Ferrar at Little Gidding, and the Caroline divines. Cornwall was remote, but there is evidence from this period of the continuance of craftsmanship and artistic feeling uninterrupted by religious change. We see a brief flowering in the later woodwork at Landulph, Lanreath, Talland, St. Winnow, St. Ives and other places. At Altarnun there are two paintings of about 1620, one depicting the administration of the Eucharist or the Last Supper. The interesting point is that two lighted candles are shown on the table, and this was taken in the time of the ritual judgments of last century as evidence of the use of such ornaments in the Church at that date.

By this time the Church of England had, for thousands of the devout, become as the Catholic Church. Examination of the episcopal and parish registers demonstrates the continuity of working of the machinery of the diocese. Visitations, confirmations, ordinations, the installation of parish clergy, marriages, christenings, burials proceeded without break through all the changes from Henry to Charles I. The sonorous liturgy had speeded the retreat of the Cornish language, and welded the men of the county more firmly to the rest of England. Here and there the old devout ways of private recitation of the offices – morning and evening prayer – were carried on. Is it by a kind of insight as to the continuity of the Church in essentials of ministry and creed that the question can be answered – why were the Cornish, so addicted to their Latin mass and the unreformed faith, so loyal to Church and king in the Civil War?

At the outbreak of that struggle, in which the policies of Charles, the peremptory attitude of Laud, the sincerity of the Puritan zealots and the clearer view of the functions of Parliament all had their share, the leading Puritan clergy in Cornwall were Charles Morton of Blisland, John Wills of Morval, Jasper Hicks of Landrake, and Thomas Peters of Mylor, brother of Hugh, chaplain to Cromwell. Laity prominent in that party were Lord Robartes of Lanhydrock, the Bullers of Morval, the Rouses of Halton, and the Boscawens of Tregothnan. They were mostly moderate Presbyterians. The actions of the king and archbishop Laud in ecclesiastical affairs pushed many into sympathy with the Puritans and Parliament who were previously moderate Churchmen.

In 1641 the majority of Cornish M.P.s – 36 out of 44 – signed a protestation to defend the reformed religion against popish innovations. This protestation was read in 202 parishes in Cornwall. With the outbreak of war an ordinance was passed by the Parliament in 1644 for the ejecting of 'scandalous ministers', that is in practice, those who did not accept or share the Puritan point of view. This ordinance was delayed in its effect so far as Cornwall was concerned, for the county, so strongly Royalist, twice threw back the Parliament forces, first at Braddock and Stratton in 1643, and again around Lostwithiel in 1644. That district in the lovely Fowey valley suffered much damage. The chapelry of St. Nighton lost its tower, battered down in the contest around Lostwithiel, where the Royalists had their adversaries surrounded. The town's church was badly handled, the Parliament men baptizing a horse in the font, and attempting to blow up the building with Royalist prisoners inside.

With the capitulation to Fairfax of the king's army at Tresillian Bridge in 1645 the county and Church lay open to the rule of Parliament. Bishop Ralph Brownrigg of Exeter was expelled – probably he never actually took up his residence, owing to the war – and retired to live quietly in Berkshire where he died sequestered in December 1659. The cathedral chapter was deprived, the Prayer book was forbidden (1645) and the ejection of parochial clergy who refused to take the Covenant began in the summer of 1646. Some 72 priests were unacceptable to the county committee which was responsible for this work. This was a high, but not the highest, proportion among the counties of England. Some clergy submitted to the Parliament willingly; some unwillingly for the sake of their flocks.

The county committee was active in the deprivations and the appointment of suitable ministers ordered after a Presbyterian or Independent manner. It consisted of Stephen Revell, a solicitor, John Moyle, and Captain William Braddon. Each deprived priest was to be awarded one-fifth of the revenue of his sequestered living. In practice this was not seldom withheld or delayed. Hugh Colmer, rector of Ladock, was reduced to destitution and his parishioners sent him their children to be taught till even this was forbidden by law. Dr. Peterson, who was dean of Exeter and rector of St. Breoke, where he resided and was well loved, was harshly ejected late one evening, even though a petition of his parishioners pleaded for his restoration. Richard Tucker was a widower with eight small children. On his deprivation, neighbours sheltered him and his family; he was later allowed to hold a small and poor living. Thomas Flavell of Mullion, having been outspoken in the king's cause, was searched for to be hanged, but hid himself till the scare was over, and was allowed to live in the parsonage without income. He vowed he would let his beard grow till the king came back, which he accordingly did.

The list of clergy, thus removed from their canonical sphere of labour, can be studied in Walker's *Sufferings of the Clergy*, compiled from contemporary sources. It should be borne in mind in reading this work, and the corresponding work on the other side, that feelings ran high and anything like comprehension or tolerance had yet to be achieved.

The place of a deprived man was taken perhaps by some local pastor who had satisfied the Puritans and agreed to be responsible for service in another church. Thus Robert Jago, vicar of Wendron, was awarded £40–£50 for preaching at other places as well. John Braddon of Otterham had £40 in 1647 for services at St. Mabyn. In other parishes the benefices were filled by nominees of Parliament ordained in a Presbyterian mode but who in some cases were unlearned and inexperienced men.

Throughout the period of the Commonwealth there was a shortage of ministers and a wide neglect of the communion. The county had little enthusiasm for Presbyterianism. Its mystical turn of mind found more in common with George Fox and the Quakers, whose first mission to Cornwall occurred in 1655. Another piece of evidence is that the county ministers were not, it seems, organized as elsewhere into a Presbyterian 'classis' of a strict kind. There survive the minutes of the Cornwall classis formed in 1655. It was a voluntary association of divines, consisting of 23 ministers and 3 laymen (who were soon afterwards ordained). It met in three divisions, St. Agnes–Veryan, Bodmin, and Looe–Boscastle. Later meetings regulated the order to be followed in making ministers, and disciplinary matters affecting the congregations. It was, however, but a shade of the strict regimen found elsewhere.

Parliament moved further against the traditional order of the Church of England. In August 1653 came another ordinance, permitting civil marriage before a Justice of the Peace. Lay registers of births and deaths were to be appointed. In Truro John Bagwell was appointed for this purpose, and the first civil marriage then follows, in November 1653, before Jacob Daniell as J.P., between Richard Garland, of St. Veep, and Mary Bramshaw, of Veryan. This civil function was not at all to the liking of the people generally, who often asked for the marriage to be performed again before the minister. In the register of St. Mary's, Launceston is the comment '27 Nov. 1655. Hereafter follow marriages by laymen, according to the profaneness and giddyness of the times, without precedent or example in any Christian Kingdom or Commonwealth from the Birth of Christ unto this very year 1655'.

Much iconoclasm in the churches took place at this time. Many stained windows were smashed in 1645–46, at St. Agnes and elsewhere, for the windows had survived earlier 'reforms' almost unscathed. The 'Raylings' – that is, the roodscreen, at St. Ives was taken down, and the organ destroyed. The larger pipes long did duty in the town as rainwater shoots! At Launceston, too, the organ was taken down; some parts lingered in the vestry till a new organ was built there about 1720. The Puritans did not object to organs as such, but to the sometimes frivolous accompaniment to the church service associated with them. It seemed to them more in accordance with the grave worship of God that simplicity and purely vocal singing should be found in the churches.

Buildings remained unfinished or neglected – the tower of St. Mewan to this day is incomplete for this reason, and not, as local tradition would have it, through the activity of the devil taking away the stones at night! At Mevagissey too the tower became ruinous at this time, and the bells were sold.

As the power of Cromwell increased and that of Parliament declined, feeling once in support of the latter slowly turned back to the Royalist cause. Lord Robartes of Lanhydrock, who had long been one of the foremost supporters of the Presbyterian parliament cause, began to change his mind. He was summoned before the Council and ordered to live elsewhere, as well as finding two securities of £20,000 each for his good behaviour.

With the introduction of military government in 1655 and the triumph of Independence over Presbyterianism this realignment of loyalties proceeded more rapidly. It was with relief and hope that the inhabitants of the towns and villages of Cornwall welcomed the news of the king's Restoration, and with him the system of the Anglican Church.

4

Restoration – The Eighteenth Century

THE BELLS THAT JOYFULLY RANG THE RETURN OF CHARLES II to the throne in the summer of 1660 also heralded the resumption by the Anglican Church of the position it enjoyed before the 'usurpation'; its privileges and rights of a temporal kind were soon also restored to it.

The Exeter bells rang out again to welcome the arrival of the new bishop, John Gauden. He was reputedly the author of the *Eikon Basilike,* and had been consecrated by Juxon, who had attended Charles I at the scaffold. His entry into Exeter was something of a triumph since he was accompanied by several coaches and some hundreds of horsemen. The palace having been used during the Commonwealth as a sugar refinery, Dr. Gauden sought lodgings elsewhere. He found his cathedral divided by 'the Babylonish wall' built to separate dissident Puritans from one another's devotions in service time!

The Commonwealth rule of Presbyterians and Independents, though short in term of years, left a deep mark on the religious susceptibilities of the nation and of Cornwall. The Puritan and Anglican theologies and ethos had become hardened during the struggle. Great damage had naturally been done to the administration of the Church and to the church buildings. There was a widespread ignorance of, and prejudice against, the liturgy. The Puritan interpretation of Sunday as the Sabbath had become the norm, and its suspicion of the use of art and music and beauty in the service of God was (and is) shared by many who would not own the description Puritan in their theology.

One of the first acts of bishop Gauden was to ordain 44 priests and deacons in his cathedral to fill up the vacant benefices in Devon and Cornwall. The liturgy began to be used again in its pre-Commonwealth form, while in the meantime a conference of Puritan and Anglican divines met at the Savoy to discuss their differences and to try to find a way of compromise and reconciliation. It speedily became apparent that neither side would give way. A few minor concessions were made by the Anglicans, but their conviction was that the Puritans' objections were symptomatic of a completely different approach to the Christian faith. Consequently the new Prayer book issued in 1662 represented the victorious Anglicanism in no mood for further attempts at conciliation.

The book of 1662 was to come into use on 24th August, by which time those who had not subscribed, nor regularized their orders were to be deprived of their benefices. In the eyes of strict Anglicans the nominees of Parliament who had been ministering in the parishes were uncanonically instituted, their claim to the tithes was illegal, and their Presbyterian or Independent ordination invalid.

About 50 ministers of Cornish parishes of the Puritan stamp felt conscientiously unable to subscribe to the new Book and the old ceremonies. They resigned their livings, or were deprived. Some of the parish priests ejected in 1646 by the Parliament Committee were still alive, and were restored to their old place. Those now deprived in 1662 were in many cases serious and able men, whose story we must take up in the following chapter, where the two kinds of dissent from the Established Church will find description.

The restored clergy found their position difficult. In June 1660 there was a petition to the Lords from 20 Cornish incumbents asking for the restoration of their tithe. In 1663 Thomas Flavell, the Royalist vicar of Mullion desired the help of the ecclesiastical authorities for the reformation of his churchwardens, who refused to supply the bread and wine for the Whitsunday communion. Mevagissey pleaded in 1665 that the bells had been embezzled, and sold to one Grouden, a Quaker, during the interregnum. Denis Grenville, the non-resident rector of Kilkhampton, complained that his curate there had to officiate without a surplice to please the 'dowbaked' parishioners. It would seem that the spirit of 'lame Eusebius Paget' lived on. St. Mary's, Truro, spent £6 7s. for two surplices in 1662, and a large sum was needed for church repairs.

Bishop Seth Ward's Visitation in 1665 disclosed many problems. Some of the clergy presented – i.e. reported – parishioners for irreverence in church or non-attendance at the services. At St. Columb Major, for instance, there were 'many who do not kneel at prayers, or stand up at the Gospel, nor bow at the name of Jesus'. At Helland, after notice had been given of St. Peter's day, and a reproof to the parishioners for not coming to church as was expected on holy days, Nicholas Opy stood up and interrupted with 'loud words'. This gentleman 'doth always wear his hat in the time of preaching'; yet he was not a dissenter, as his child was baptized at Bodmin.

Several parishes were filled by men who were only in deacon's orders as was common in medieval days. Robert Triggs, ordered deacon 4th March, 1663, was instituted to Sithney the day following. John Sharp, vicar of Lostwithiel remained a deacon for a year and four months while incumbent.

In 1666 Ward issued to the vicar and churchwardens of Crowan a commission to draw up a table of seating, so that the parishioners, who had sat anywhere during the Commonwealth and had squabbled over their pews, might sit in order and precedence. A few years later a Cornish incumbent wrote to ask where the clergy should obtain hoods, ordered by the bishop in 1670 to be worn, stating they were never used save at universities and cathedrals, and that scarcely anyone in Cornwall had one. Would tippets do instead? Obviously there was a great deal of sorting out to be done, involving many questions and much strife.

Some irreverence sprang from a dissent from the church's principles, provoked by the repressive legislation carried through by a triumphant and Anglican Parliament and king. This legislation was aimed, as we shall see, at rendering powerless the remaining Puritan opinion and preventing public worship in their manner. The Quakers of the period were much given to a silent or spoken protest in service time. The grave figure with the tall hat – they refused to uncover in church – would rise and stand looking severely at the officiant, perhaps quoting some text which seemed apposite, till removed without ceremony. More irreverence originated in the wide ignorance of the liturgy and the Anglican way of worship. Consequently, in 1667, at his primary Visitation bishop Anthony Sparrow included in his charge strong teaching on the Eucharist, church order, obedience to the true and avoidance of false teachers. 'Steadfast in the faith – as the Catholic and Apostolic Church hath believed and declared.' To further this knowledge of Anglican ways Sparrow published his *Rationale* on the Prayer book in 1676, which went through several editions. In this book the bishop displays a knowledge of ancient liturgy in his explanation of the Common prayer, and commends a number of ceremonies, such as kissing the Gospel book at the end of the lection in the communion. Sparrow's census of the diocese in 1672 showed that in Cornwall there were 65,811 conformists, 842 dissenters and 67 papists.

With the fresh energies flowing in the Church of England attempts were made to restore something of decency in the bleak churches by the replacement of ornaments removed or destroyed during the Commonwealth. The communion tables which had been placed altar-wise at the east end of the chancel and railed in before the Civil War, were so placed once more. At Altarnun is a splendid set of rails stretching right across the church, dated 1684, and a set at North Petherwin (now at the back of the church) dated 1685. Both these are in a sturdy country style of craftsmanship with a simple dignity. Breage replaced the rails in 1693, and Antony in 1698 paid Robert Greet £4 10s. for 'Realing the Communion Table'.

Many gifts of altar plate were also made at this time, although the Elizabethan communion vessels had remained in use for the infrequent administration of communion under the Parliament rule. Something like 17 pieces of plate date from the reign of Charles II alone.

Perhaps the most striking symbol of the revival of Anglicanism is to be seen in the founding of the church at Falmouth. It was at Pendennis Castle that the last Royalist stand on the Cornish mainland was made, and the town had been growing by reason of the wide harbour. In 1661 Sir Peter Killigrew obtained from Charles II and others money for the founding of a new church for the place, to which a charter had been given by the same king. The foundation of the church was laid on 29th August, 1662, and the building is in a mixed style of Gothic Renaissance. Seth Ward consecrated the church in 1665, a parish being annexed to it, taken out of the old parish of Budock. Falmouth church stands as a memorial and a thanksgiving for the Civil War and the Restoration. Its dedication to 'King Charles' reflects the view of many a devout Anglican that in spite of his political unwisdom the execution of the king was at least partly on account of his identification with that Church.

Between 1686 and 1702 galleries were erected in Falmouth church and an organ in 1702. This must have been among the earliest post-Restoration instruments in Cornwall. Launceston obtained one in 1723, and other churches followed suit no doubt. But a great many Cornish parish churches contented themselves with a group of singers in the west gallery and a pitch pipe to give the note for the metrical psalms which at the time would be about all that was sung in the service.

The old Cornish family of Trelawny, of Trelawne near Pelynt, furnished the bishop of Bristol in James II's reign. Jonathan Trelawny was one of the seven bishops imprisoned in the Tower as a result of their petition against the order to read the Declaration of Indulgence. This would have allowed to nonconformist and papist religious freedom, but was aimed at helping the Roman Catholics without consent of Parliament.

The policy of James inevitably led to his abdication, in 1688. Thomas Lamplugh, the bishop of Exeter, exhorted his clergy not to receive William of Orange and to remain loyal in their sworn allegiance to James, but transferred his allegiance to William the moment he was on the throne! His clergy were not slow to follow his example. Only two, James Beauford, rector of Lanteglos-by-Camelford, and Thomas Polwhele, vicar of Newlyn East, refused to renounce their sworn obedience and as non-jurors resigned their benefices. Denis Grenville, dean of Durham and one-time rector of Kilkhampton, gave up his preferments and followed his sovereign into exile. It was Grenville who strove so hard to introduce a weekly Eucharist in all cathedrals, and to increase the frequency with which that ordinance was celebrated in the parish churches.

Trelawny was translated to Exeter at the time of the abdication, and during his episcopate made Trelawne his usual place of residence. Here he held his court and performed many ordinations in the chapel which he consecrated in 1701. Out of 78 ordinations 53 were performed in Cornwall – 35 at Trelawne and 18 in the parish church of Pelynt. For a while it was as though Cornwall had its own bishop again.

In 1707 he was once more translated, this time to Winchester, where his primary charge, which of course would represent his views while in Cornwall also, speaks of well developed Church principles 'and the certainty, nay perhaps the necessity, of our Hierarchy' in ordaining to the ministry. On his death the body was brought back to Cornwall and the pastoral staff carried before him is preserved in Pelynt church.

There was a close identification in Cornwall of Tory interest and the Church. At the Revolution and the coming of William the Whig principles were carried to victory, and the expulsion of the non-juring clergy was regarded as a declaration of 'war' against the Tory high-churchmen. Party spirit again raged. On the death of William the Church had a brief interlude of popularity. At this time the great Societies S.P.C.K. and S.P.G. were founded, and there was a new enthusiasm for the Church of England in many parishes. In towns and large villages 'Societies' for the spiritual life, or for the reformation of manners, might be found. As late as 1743 there was such a society in St. Ives, from which, as we shall see, a new meaning came into Cornish religion.

When Anne died in 1714, James III was actually proclaimed king in St. Columb marketplace! There was considerable support for the Jacobite cause, and the notorious high church and Tory Dr. Sacheverel – whose nominal sentence for sedition was taken as a virtual acquittal – was commemorated in an inscription in St. Just church as the preserver of safety and protection for the Church of England!

There was a good deal of activity in the parishes. A pulpit sounding board and screen were erected at Madron by parson Rowe in Queen Anne's time. In 1706 the rector of Truro, having outstayed his time away from the parish to take his wife to Bath, was duly brought up before the bishop's court and admonished to keep his full residence. Several benefactors gave the same church money to provide for the preaching of funeral sermons – a protestant reflection of the earlier desire for requiems in the old days; there was a list of eleven such sermons, to be preached annually, in 1699.

From the reign of Anne can be traced the beginnings of the gradual rise in the world of the Anglican parson. We are on the threshold of the great days of the rectory and its family, married off into the ranks of the lesser gentry, the hard work in the parish being performed by some underpaid curate who might, if he were lucky, be given some small living only after many years as an assistant or substitute to an absentee priest. Parsonage houses of a more substantial kind began to be built. That at St. Mary's, Penzance, dates from 1701, while at Linkinhorne the vicarage bears the date 1725 and the initials of George Jeffrey the then vicar.

In 1727 St. Gennys vicarage was described as of stone and cob, covered with 'raggs'. It contained six rooms; one had a deal floor, but none was ceiled or wainscotted. This house was new-built in 1734.

A fund for poor clergymen's widows and orphans was opened, and at Bodmin, in June 1737, a meeting made a collection of over £200 for this relief fund. By 1755 there was a fund to help necessitous clergy, with clerical representatives annually elected. It was operating as late as 1848.

The work of S.P.C.K. and S.P.G., founded at the turn

of the century, extended into the parishes through the agency of books and tracts distributed by local clergy appointed as agents. John Penrose, vicar of St. Gluvias, was one such, and records in his diary the receiving by sea of parcels of tracts. In 1752 his whole order of books from S.P.C.K. amounted to 2,892.

In the same year the bishop in a letter asked for a collection to be made for S.P.G., and Penrose diligently preached on the subject, and collected in the town and parish for its funds. It is not without interest to detail the sums raised locally:

	£	s.	d.
Penryn	17	6	3½
Budock	1	1	0
St. Gluvias	5	19	6
Mabe	1	1	0
Mylor	3	18	6
Mawnan	1	0	0
	£30	6	3½

The place of the Church in the life of a country gentleman may perhaps be gauged from the diary of George Browne, who was registrar to the archdeaconry court of Cornwall in the middle 18th century. He attended church at Blisland most Sundays, usually in the morning. Three or four times a year he made his communion. He went to church on Good Friday, spent Easter Eve quietly at home, and was at the morning service on Easter Day 1771; he does not specifically mention the communion being celebrated on that day. He carefully records with obvious interest who took the service or preached, and the changes of incumbencies in the neighbourhood, as well as the frequent dinners he had with the local parsons. With the vicar and mayor of Bodmin he goes collecting for the poor in January 1776.

However, the opening of the Georgian era in 1715 had ushered in the ascendancy of Whig and Latitudinarian principles. Henceforth no parson who was a Tory, or of the 'High Church' school in politics, was likely to be made a bishop. Convocation was suppressed in 1717, and a deadly sleep had begun slowly to paralyse the nation's soul.

In the teaching of the Church there echoed the controversies with the Deists and others, whose appeal to reason and the natural order rendered it imperative that Christian theology should seem to be consonant with them. But this was not the best fare for unlettered miners and labourers in the parishes of Cornwall. Dignity, reason, the seemliness of worship left a great gap in the souls of the humble. The official Church was preoccupied with the needs of the great minds and of the leading families, immersed in cultural activities which bore much fruit but left the lower classes unmoved. To say the Church was out of touch would not be true – it was deeply integrated with those who ruled and thought. At the local level law and administration were in its hands through the vestry and wardens. But the clergy's relation with their flock was often that of squire and magistrate only, and their interests remote from the cares of the lowly.

The roll of eighteenth century clergy who made their mark on culture and science is not short. Some were in the forefront of their chosen study. William Borlase, rector of Ludgvan, historian and antiquary, for instance stands head and shoulders above others of his day. There was Charles Peters, rector of St. Mabyn 1726–75. He was recognized as the finest Hebrew scholar in Europe, and published a *Dissertation on the Book of Job* in 1751. He was generous to a fault, and entertained every Sunday at his table some of the poor of his parish. Malachi Hitchens, vicar of St. Hilary 1775–1809, previously assisted at the Royal Observatory and constructed the first *Nautical Almanac* in 1767 and succeeding years as a computer. William Gregor, rector of Creed, discovered a magnetic sand, calling it 'manaccanite', in the course of his researches into the minerals of Cornwall. Jonathan Toup, rector of St. Martin-by-Looe 1750–85 gained an international reputation as critic, Greek scholar and philologist. Robert Walker, vicar of St. Winnow 1781–1834, pioneered agricultural research with his friend Sir Charles Vinnicombe Penrose, introduced several new breeds of pigs into the county, endeavoured to improve the lot of the labourers, and was the acknowledged 'father' of the Parliamentarian Reformers.

Such men, however active, were in pastoral touch only with a section of the population. In Cornwall the mining industry was beginning to attract those huge crowds which characterized it at the beginning of the new century. Many of the new centres of industry lay far from the old parish churches, and villages grew up four and five miles away from the 'churchtown' in some parishes. Nevertheless, at the middle of the century, there was still a faithfulness to the parish church surprisingly strong here and there. At St. Just, William Borlase's other living, there was commonly a congregation of a thousand in the morning, the church then being furnished with galleries.

Clear evidence of the drift of things in the latter half of the eighteenth century may be found by comparing the Replies made by the parochial clergy to the Questionnaires sent out by the bishops in preparation for their Visitations. The first series of 1744, asked for by bishop Clagget, shows that there was a daily service at St. Ives and a few other places; several others had 'prayers', that is, morning and evening prayer, on Wednesdays and Fridays, as well as two services on Sundays. In towns the holy communion was celebrated monthly as a rule, while in country parishes it may have been but three or four times a year. Catechizing of the young, according to the rubric, was performed in many places, often in the summer only.

The numbers attending at the altar show a progressive decline all through the eighteenth century. Take as an example the parish of Padstow, where the influence of Methodism was not strong enough to mask the process. In 1744 the attendance was normally 100. In 1779 the figure was 80, and by 1821 it had dropped to 60–70.

A similar decline is noticeable in the number of clergy residing in their parishes. At the beginning of the century, as we saw, residence was insisted upon and an incumbent who was absent from his parish for more than three months was admonished. The whole question of pluralities and non-residence was a continuing abuse, inherited from the Middle Ages, which the Reformation did nothing to abolish but merely modified. The eighteenth century shed its own murky colour upon it. The available returns for the 1744 Visitation show there were 110 clergy who resided, with eight curates resident in parishes where the incumbent was an absentee. Thirty-six did not reside, and nine resided outside the parish, but so near as to be able to serve it.

The returns of 1779, however, show that the number of non-residents had risen to 57, with only 89 living in their parishes; the increase in those who did not reside, but left the work to ill-paid curates, is very marked. In spite of admonitions and legislation, the returns for 1821 show the position was at its worst with 82 resident and 63 non-resident. It was in this period that the influence of Methodism was most marked, and to its opening story we must now turn.

The reaction against the over emphasis on reason in religion came about with an appeal to intuition and the feelings; to the Spirit of God rather than duty towards him. The new zealousness had many founts. One independent source was found in the ministry of George Thomson, vicar of St. Gennys near Bude, 1732–82. This man had had a remarkable, but not particularly spiritual, career as a chaplain before he came to this windswept place on the north coast. Soon after his arrival at St. Gennys he was converted to a new seriousness, by a recurrent dream of his imminent death. This change in outlook would be about 1735, several years before the 'heart warming' experience enjoyed by the Wesley brothers. Through friendship with James Hervey, Thomson became known to George Whitefield, another member of Wesley's 'Holy Club', and a fervent priest evangelist. Whitefield preached in St. Gennys church more than once. John Bennet, a neighbouring curate in charge of the isolated parishes of North Tamerton, Laneast and Tresmere, in north Cornwall, also found a new earnestness in his ministry by the example of Thomson, and became a disciple of his.

The vicar of St. Gennys, not content with urging his own people to a truer religion, preached around the district to the disgust of his clerical neighbours. The name of 'Methodist' – then a common term for anyone in earnest about religion – was applied to his followers, though it is doubtful how far Thomson had any links with Wesley's people at that point. The vicar of Marhamchurch complained in 1744 to the bishop about Thomson's 'circumforaneous vociferations', and the worthy itinerant was admonished to confine his preaching henceforth to his own parish. John Wesley and his brother Charles, as well as Whitefield, preached at St. Gennys and a few other north Cornish churches in the first years of their work in the county.

What first brought the Wesleys to Cornwall seems to have been the news of the religious society at St. Ives, and realization of the numbers and need of industrial Cornwall. Charles Wesley arrived first in 1743, preceding his brother by some three weeks. It should be mentioned that both the Wesleys and Whitefield were Anglican priests and that the object of the Methodist mission was to evangelize, not to form a new sect, and to supplement, not supplant the Anglican system. It was pressed upon those who responded to the earnest exhortations to 'flee from the wrath to come' that they were to go to the parish church for service on Sundays and for communion. The Methodist devotions of those days never clashed with the time of the church service, and John Wesley and his helpers constantly attended the local church. The regulations for Wesley's assistants, or travelling preachers, also commended loyalty to the Anglican Church, or, in the case of the few dissenters, to their own meeting. John Wesley himself, in the *Journal* records of his thirty-one visits to Cornwall, mentions his attendance at the churches of St. Ives, on both weekdays and Sundays, Zennor, Redruth, Wendron and Sancreed. Indeed, it was for long the universal custom for Methodists to be among the most regular attendants at their parish churches.

There was a concentration of preaching in the west, for it was primarily to the mining population, so neglected, that Wesley turned. The names St. Just, Camborne, Redruth, Gwennap, Breage, Sithney, Crowan and Gwinear are names of mining parishes and of frequent occurrence in the *Journal*. The converts were joined in a local 'society', which was the fundamental unit of Methodism, and led by class leaders and exhorters recruited from the district towards a true fear of God. The societies began to multiply, and houses were opened for the Methodist preaching.

The opening of the Wesleys' work in Cornwall was quite unconsciously ill-timed. The native caution of the Cornish in dealing with strangers and the prevailing political conditions rendered it considerable disservice. The first visits of the Wesley brothers in 1743 coincided with a period of tension that was particularly strong in the extreme west owing to preparations being made for war by France. A time of unofficial hostilities led on to the declaration of war against France in March 1744. Privateers had already taken prisoner three of the principal Mount's Bay fishermen, and popular opinion clamoured for the protection of a man-o'-war to protect the bay. A rumour, started up in London, gained ground that there was a large store of arms laid up in the Penzance district. One of the local magistrates, Walter Borlase (brother of the antiquary, and vicar of Madron), discovered that many of the small arms from a wrecked privateer, the *Charming Molly*, which had run aground near St. Michael's Mount, were missing and others had been sold to those known to be disaffected and Jacobite in sympathy.

This ferment reached its peak in 1745, and as it grew Wesley in all innocence began to proclaim his message and to gather his societies. He concentrated his attention on those whose reliability was most in doubt, the miners, who in their poverty had rioted oftentimes in the past. In the considerable opposition ranged against Methodism in its first years can be traced the confused idea that the societies were being formed to prepare the way for the invasion of the country. An amusing letter written in 1745 by a certain Mr. Baron to the Duke of Newcastle expresses the widely-held opinion that the Cornish Methodists were in liaison with the Pretender – an idea which was apparently held by all the gentry of West Cornwall at the time, as Wesley was informed.

The *Journal* records of the visit of John Wesley in 1743, 1744 and 1745 are full of references to the violent mobbing of the societies, mostly in the ports such as St. Ives and Falmouth, and the wrecking of the room at St. Ives where the Methodists met. Wesley names as principals in the stirring up of mob violence the two clergy of St. Ives, Symonds and Hoblyn. Attempts were made to seize him and his helpers as pressed men for the service of the army.

Amid this violence and mobbing John Wesley moved with a calmness and openness which tamed the most vicious opponent and delivered the Methodists from bodily harm. It was at Falmouth, in July 1745, that an oft-quoted incident took place which clearly displays the boldness of Wesley in the face of danger. He had gone to pay a sick call at a house near the harbour when a multitude, hearing he was there, surrounded the place. Wesley was in an inner room separated from the passage only by a wood partition. In the passage and about the door, which they had wrenched from its hinges after battering it with stones, was a crowd including the crews of some privateers in the harbour.

The inner door soon yielded to the thrust of brawny sailor muscles, and the mob surged into the room. Wesley calmly stood in the midst, and spoke to them. Unharmed he made his way to the street, to be met by 'Mr. Thomas, a clergyman,' who, with one of the town's aldermen, rebuked the crowd at using a stranger thus. Wesley was able to get away by boat to Penryn, and pick up his horse, which had been sent on by the alderman, at that place.

By 1747 the Pretender's threat had vanished – so had the opposition to Methodist preaching. Wesley himself noted of St. Ives in that year – 'This is now a peaceable, nay, honourable station. They give us good words almost in every place.' No rioting on any large scale occurred thereafter. A few places where Methodism was newly introducing gathered mobs, but there was little violence in the county as a whole. Petty opposition and mischief-making of course was common.

In the years that followed the growth of Methodism was phenomenal, especially after 1780. In the late eighteenth century the introduction of efficient steam power meant that mines could be worked on a larger scale, and huge numbers daily assembled to labour above and below ground. When Methodism had found acceptance among a few miners, its rapid spread among the crowds was assured. Prayer meetings and devotions in the depths, preaching from the count house steps, so wove mining and Methodism that they became all but synonymous terms.

The growth of Methodism was not a steady progress. There were periods of recession, and periods when great waves or 'revivals' swept the countryside, gathering in hundreds in a few weeks. These 'Revivals', which were excitable and in some eyes extravagant campaigns, broke out at intervals of roughly sixteen years – in 1764, 1782, 1799, 1814 – known as the 'Great Revival', and 1831. Each of these had its origin in a mining parish; by comparison the eastern part of the county was untouched. According to the old West Cornwall circuit book the largest societies in 1774 were Gwennap, with 146 members and Redruth with 128 members. By 1799 the largest societies were Redruth with 754 and Tuckingmill with 459. These figures relate only to formally admitted members. Countless others would be 'hearers' of the preaching, so that in many parishes a large majority of the inhabitants came under Methodist influence in one way or another.

The first places of meeting of the Methodist societies were no doubt private houses. There is the mention in the 1744 returns of local Methodists meeting at the house of John Nance in St. Ives 'at unseasonable hours' – that is, at times which were not those of the usual church services. A similar note is made concerning the house of Matthew Thomas at Zennor. But at St. Just there was an unlicensed house 'appropriated to the Methodists'. Thereafter Methodist preaching-houses (Wesley's term for them) became common. They were humble places, furnished only with a desk and benches, as we gather from the old account book of the St. Just society, where there are entries in 1766 – 'To Thomas Pearce for painting the Desk, and mending the windows – as by Bill, 5s. 5d.', and in 1772, 'repairing the Binches, 1s. 0d.'

The mention of an 'unlicensed house' is a reminder that the early Methodists, reckoning themselves to be loyal to the Church of England, disdained to avail themselves of the Toleration Acts, since that would involve them in a profession of dissent, by which assemblies other than those of the Church were protected. This refusal to license the house rendered the Methodist meetings liable to disturbance by mobs, and the magistrates had no legal authority to protect them even if they so desired.

By 1785 the loyalty to the Church of England had become blurred and licences were taken out with a profession of protestant dissent. In the St. Just account book under the year 1785 is the entry – 'to Expenses and horse Iren when before the Commishenors aboute the preaching House, 2s. 0d.' Places of meeting where more than twenty assembled had to be registered with the bishop, the archdeacon, or justices at Quarter Sessions. Long lists survive of the meeting houses of protestant dissenters of all kinds from the end of the eighteenth century onwards, from whence it is possible to extract the Methodist chapels only by a knowledge of the names of the people submitting the application.

In what way, we may ask, did the more earnest clergy view the remarkable effects of the down-to-earth preaching of the Methodists? By the mid-century there was a little group of parish priests interpreting religion in an evangelical manner and labouring devotedly in their parishes. In the first years Thomson and Bennet had welcomed the Wesleys, but an estrangement began to take place between them. The reasons become clear as we follow the ministry of the most illustrious of them all – Samuel Walker, curate of Truro 1746–61. This man was of such spiritual stature that John Wesley spoke of him with deep respect, deferred to his opinions, and never preached in Truro while he was there. At St. Mary's he was in charge for an absentee incumbent, St. John Elliot, who resided nearby at Ladock, and whom it appears he converted.

Walker gathered round himself societies similar to

those of the Methodists, but strictly under his own care. To the townspeople he constantly taught the Gospel, finding it set out in Bible and Prayer book, and upheld the teaching of the Church, with prayers on saints' days, and frequent sermons, and preparation for communion, all warmed with fervent devotion and zeal. In his societies Walker was guide, adviser, confessor and friend.

He associated with himself other local clergy of like mind in a 'Clerical Club', which began to meet monthly in 1750. By 1752 it appears from the diary of John Penrose, one of the members, that the three Walkers (Samuel of Truro, James of St. Agnes, and Robert of Lawhitton), Penrose of St. Gluvias, Michel of Veryan, Thomas of St. Clement, a Mr. Carthew, and St. John Elliot of Ladock made up the little circle of devout clergy. In later years the curates Cooper of Cubert, Vowler and Philp of St. Agnes, and perhaps Philipps vicar of Gwennap were members or were associated with the Club.

These men all took their cue from Walker of Truro in their relations with the growing Methodist societies in the towns and villages of Cornwall.

It seemed to the earnest curate of Truro that Wesley had set out on a wrong course both in practice and in teaching. Walker and the clergy who thought like him tended to interpret the Anglican formularies in a Calvinistic direction, to press the sovereignty of God, and they saw the assurance proper to a Christian in the settled mind and will which God gave. Wesley, on the other hand, was an Arminian in that he upheld the view Christ died for all, and that all may be saved, as against only the elect. Walker also suspected that in time Wesley's choice of lay preachers would be embarrassing as they began to aspire to the ministry. A correspondence began between the Wesleys and Walker, in which more sympathy became apparent between Charles and the curate of Truro than between him and John Wesley.

The Calvinistic-Arminian controversy came to a head outside Cornwall in 1770, but its repercussions were felt in the county, and the two wings of the Evangelical Revival henceforth went their own ways. The regular clergy laboured in their parishes, finding there a sphere of work sufficient for their energies. Some of them were effective and beloved priests. Penrose followed his mentor Walker's societies with one at Penryn as did Michel at Veryan. When Walker went away after being admonished by the bishop for curtailing the funeral service for a notorious profligate, Penrose took alarm lest he was going over to the dissenters! Thomas Wills had huge success at St. Agnes, where he was curate, the church being so full when he preached that he could hardly get through to the desk. In 1778 he gave up his Anglican ministry to enter Lady Huntingdon's Connexion and took part in the ordination of her ministers.

Other men maintained an evangelical succession in Cornish parishes. There was Samuel Furly, sen., rector of Roche 1766–95, friend of Wesley in earlier days, Thomas Biddulph of Padstow, 1771–90, and his successor William Rawlings, vicar 1790–1836, while others will come before our notice later. From this earnest evangelical background came Henry Martyn 1781–1812, son of a follower of Walker, who became a missionary in Persia and died in that country.

The Methodists began to find in their own system a complete expression of the Christian religion. The parish clergy, where not actually hostile, were not well disposed to their parishioners who attended the 'preaching'. Often the lay preachers explicitly or implicitly criticized the ordinary clergy. Memories of the Puritan regime remained in the background, awakening fear that the Church might again be endangered. Squire and parson, if not using their influence to deter their tenants from joining the society, at least held all the offices in the parish church in their hands.

Methodism, however, was the poor man's religion, later that of the new middle class. It was staffed by ordinary folk. The earnest miner could preach or lead class, the local shopkeeper might be trustee or steward. The chapel pulpit became the training ground for further things, religious and political.

Methodists began to tire of the uncongenial link with the parish church, where to them religion seemed cold and unreal. The diary of Elizabeth Harper, a Methodist of Redruth, shows how she becomes indifferent to churchgoing, not by any opposition, but by the amount of time spent on a Sunday attending both church and chapel. This was in 1766 and following years. Then, as time went on, the Methodists began to desire the sacraments at the hands of their preachers in the chapels. After 1786 Wesley had to give way and allow the holding of Methodist services at the same time as the service in the parish church in places where the incumbent was a Calvinist or hostile to the Methodist preaching. In his last years Wesley set apart a handful of his helpers to administer the sacraments in the societies in America, then in Scotland, and finally in England. This plan did not meet with general favour, and after Wesley's death in 1791 the Conference of the preachers allowed any society which wished to have the sacraments of baptism and the Lord's Supper to apply to Conference for permission, and any preacher in full connexion was allowed to minister them without any further commissioning.

The story of Methodism need not be followed further at this point. After the death of Wesley other influences were at work. Methodism divided and took on a more distinctly non-conforming attitude, though never truly dissenting as other separate groups did.

The effect of the Methodist movement on the Church of England was profound. 'Methodism was born in song', and society devotions were rendered attractive by the hymns and the melodies which accompanied them. By the middle of the eighteenth century there was a renewed interest in the singing at the parish church, which had often been a dreary business with a half-illiterate choir and a drowsy clerk. Village bands appear on the scene. In 1751 the ancient roodscreen at Madron was taken away to make room for the performance of one of Handel's oratorios. The parish bought 38 new psalm tune books in 1765 and John Courtney appears on the scene as choir trainer in 1781. At St. Erme James Trebilcock was paid £1 1s. for a year's teaching, and at Antony William Burt got the same in 1780. But at Landulph William Moon received £2 8s. 9d.; were the singers at Landulph harder to teach?

At the turn of the century a bass viol was bought at Landulph and St. Erme obtained a bassoon, and so on. No doubt the vocal and instrumental efforts were crude, but the old-time singers have left their mark on our story with their energetic practices in unheated churches to the light of a few candles painfully aspiring to render song in answer to the clerk's Sunday bidding, 'let us now sing to the praise and glory of God'.

Allied to the interest in song is the revival in ringing, and the provision of peals of bells in the churches. The sixteenth century inventories show that the usual number of bells was three, though some places like Glasney, and probably Bodmin and St. Germans, had five. In the eighteenth century there was a desire to increase the number and to ring them in peal under proper control. During the period 1712 to 1824 no less than 83 peals were cast for Cornish churches. Hardly a year passed without a tower receiving new bells, while in one year, 1767, no less than six new peals were hung. The Penningtons, of Bodmin and Stoke Climsland, cast in all 352 bells, travelling from parish to parish and setting up their furnace near the churchyard. The name Rudhall is also frequently found on

Cornish bells and there are a few other founders who cast small numbers of Cornish bells.

There was some attempt made to regulate the popular art of ringing, in which at Kenwyn 'Squire Lemon', the great mine adventurer, did not disdain to show his skill. Many towers retain their 'Ringers' Rhymes' first set up at this time, as at St. Endellion, with painted representations of the ringers in action.

Another effect of Methodism on the Church of England may be seen in an attempt to increase the accommodation in the parish churches. Helston church was rebuilt after many years' neglect in 1761, the cost being defrayed by the Earl of Godolphin. Redruth church was rebuilt, except the tower, in 1768, with galleries to accommodate the large congregation, which included at that date the local Methodists. In many other parishes galleries were erected. The main pews by this time were appropriated to various families, and the servants and poor would in many cases be relegated to a few back benches or to the galleries.

Perhaps the most striking reaction in Anglican circles lies in the revification of the old traditional theology of a distinctly high church kind. Overlaid by the popular moral and rational themes, the Catholic claims of the Church of England nonetheless remained, cherished by a few clergy and kept alive by the use of devotional works such as those of Jeremy Taylor and William Law. With a fervently emotional Methodism on all sides – in many parishes the majority of people attended the 'preaching' – thoughtful people turned back to their Prayer books and the authority of the Church and its traditions.

In the field of doctrine, the atonement, justification, assurance, sacraments and the like were all more carefully studied and taught, and distinguished from the distorted views all too current. The volumes of now unread sermons, for example, by William Sutton, 1754; Charles Peters,

1776, and others bear witness to this. The liturgy and
rubrics were defended with vigour, and there began a new
valuation of the priestly mission and authority. Faced with
the later generation of Methodist ministers, claiming to
administer the sacraments and powerful in ministry and a
sense of mission, the parish clergy took thought as to their
own standing.

Some, no doubt, fell back upon the fact of the
establishment, and challenged the unauthorized preachers
on the matter of their licences under the Toleration Acts.
But the idea of true ministry being that which possessed due
authority derived from regular succession from the apostles
again came very much to the fore, as sermon after sermon of
the time will show. There appears, however, an inadequate
idea of the Church itself in the preaching of the period. It
was for the Oxford Movement to complete the progress of
doctrine by renewing a sense of the Divine Community.

Of the Cornish school of high churchmen at the
opening of the nineteenth century – though it is perhaps
better to call it a trend rather than a school – John
Whitaker, rector of Ruan Lanyhorne, 1777–1808, was the
most prominent and deserves rescue from oblivion. He
had come from Manchester with a name for antiquarian
research, and had published a history of that town in 1771.
His literary acquaintances included Johnson and Gibbon.
From his youth Whitaker had observed with some strictness
the fasts of the Church calendar, and had absorbed the
ideas of Wheatly on the Prayer book and the ornaments of
the Church. Whether for his Arminianism, his statements
on baptismal regeneration or ministerial succession, he may
be pronounced a definite high churchman. On matters of
ceremonial his comments in his book *The Ancient Cathedral
of Cornwall* (1804) are of interest, since he laments the
disuse of the eucharistic vestments and blames the clergy
for allowing these, still ordered by the Book of Common
Prayer, he maintains, to fall into neglect. He speaks of

candles being in use in some churches, and felt that the Church of England had fallen far below the heathen in dignity of religious observance by the disuse of incense.

In character Whitaker was zealous and sincere, though not free from the place-hunting common at the time. He was forthright in rebuking the bishop of Derry for loose talk in his presence. In relations with his parishioners he brooked no nonsense, being at loggerheads with the principal ones over tithe for some years. Among his friends he numbered Richard Polwhele, the voluminous writer on Cornish matters and men, whom he influenced in a moderate high church direction. A great debt is owed by Cornish Churchmen to Whitaker, since in his work on the ancient cathedral of Cornwall he brought to light the fact that once long ago the county had bishops of its own. His work is unreadable today but it sowed the seed of the revival of the diocese of Cornwall. It is remembered of him that he had a set of false teeth – made of ebony!

The connection of the Church of England with education is clear throughout our period. There were several ancient endowed grammar schools, such as those at Truro, Launceston and Penryn, as well as a host of small private schools. These naturally instructed children in the tenets of the established Church, though towards the end of the period there were schools also supported by non-conformists.

In 1811 a meeting of the 'nobility, gentry and clergy' was held in Truro to promote interest in education, with the ideal of a school in every parish. This work was later linked with the National Society. A Central school was opened as a model in the town, and catered for the training of teachers as well as of children. In the following decades many parochial schools were founded under the protection of the National Society, which of course stood for the instruction of the young in the principles of the Church of England. The system adopted by this Society was similar to that found in the ancient grammar schools, in that there was usually only one master who taught in a large single room. A barn could be converted into a schoolroom, though many were specially built on the barn-like plan. Little furniture was demanded, and the scheme was practical in beginning the education of large numbers of children in the rudiments. The nonconformists favoured a similar system, using a single room with fixed desks.

Sunday schools were relied on where there were no day schools, and at first catered for general education as well as specifically religious teaching. One of the earliest was at St. Mary's, Truro, in 1785. By the opening of the nineteenth century there were several parishes where Sunday schools flourished. There were two in the town of Helston, one at Tintagel, two at Stratton, one at Sithney, Sancreed, Ruan Lanyhorne, and so on. This was in 1821.

In that year returns were made by the parochial clergy in preparation for bishop William Carey's Visitation. We have consequently a detailed picture of the parishes of Cornwall on the eve of the Oxford Movement and the Church revival. It is clear that the nadir of the Church's life had been reached, in spite of zeal here and there on the part of the few evangelical clergy, such as Coffin of Linkinhorne, 1780–1833, Rawlings of Padstow, 1790–1836, and Simcoe of Egloskerry, 1822–63 – this last was chemist, physician and writer, too – producing what must have been the first parochial paper in his series *Light from the West*.

The churches had become dreary through the uninspired standards of the day. The rural deans' notebooks of the opening years of the century display all too clearly the utilitarian approach to church repairs on the part of clergy and churchwardens alike. Where earlier the communion table had been graced with fine embroidered velvet, as at Camborne in 1736, often the cover was motheaten, as noted at Wendron and St. Anthony in 1809 and 1812. At Helland, in 1824, ivy was growing through the wall, presenting a large bush inside the church. At Lanteglos in 1821 the font was painted blue, and at Michaelstow the pulpit was partly of the same hue, while cabbages grew in the churchyard! Hardly a single concession to art or aesthetic consideration appears in these pages, and no reference to the preservation of the ancient woodwork which had survived.

It was time for a new wind to blow, and stir all things to revival, re-invigorating the Anglican Church to make it lay hold on its treasures with a fresh understanding of much that carelessness and hostility had led to be forgotten.

5

Separations

I – Roman Catholicism

IN 1570 POPE PAUL V ISSUED THE BULL, *REGNANS IN Excelsis*, in which he excommunicated Elizabeth, declared her deposed, and released her subjects from allegiance. It was the opening shot in a bitter campaign, partly political, partly spiritual. On the one hand was the papal Church, reinvigorated by the Council of Trent, and supported by Catholic countries, including England's enemy, Spain. On the other were the reformed provinces of England, aggressive with biblical fervour and rising national consciousness.

To the 'Roaring Bull' of 1570 the government replied the following year with a statute making it treason to publish, or act upon, any such bull. Another act in 1581 made the reconciliation of any person to Rome a treasonable matter, while the saying or hearing of the Roman mass was punishable by imprisonment. Possession of objects of devotion hallowed abroad carried the penalty of loss of goods and imprisonment. Fines were exacted for non-attendance at the Anglican services. These penal laws became more determined as tension grew and plots against the queen's life multiplied.

The 'papists' were thus on the horns of a dilemma. They could not conform without defying their own Church and spiritual father; they could not be loyal to Rome without being deemed traitors by the government. Those who held to Rome, forsook the parish church, and maintained their Roman Catholic religion secretly are known as 'recusants'.

The central figures in the story of the Cornish recusants were the members of the Arundell family and those related to them, or dependent upon them. Altogether people of papal sympathies were a minority – those of any substance totalled only about thirty – but one which it was dangerous for the government to neglect. Related by marriage to the Arundells were the Tregians of Truro and Golden, a manor near Probus. Francis Tregian, who succeeded to the estates built up by his father, being at Court used his opportunities to proselytize secure in his aristocratic Arundell connections. At Easter 1576 he took into his house at Golden a priest, Cuthbert Mayne, to minister to local Roman Catholics. Mayne was one of the first priests to land in England from Cardinal Allen's seminary at Douai, founded to train men for the English mission. At Golden Mayne ministered in secret, but went about openly as Tregian's steward.

In November 1576 Richard Grenville became sheriff of Cornwall. He was one of the thrusting, sea-minded men, protestant, hostile to the Tregians and Arundells, and jealous of their influence and wealth. Their religion gave an opening. In June 1577 the bishop was at Truro on his Visitation. Grenville descended on Golden with a large party, including many justices, on the plea of searching for a fugitive. Mayne was discovered; on his person were some devotional objects, and among his possessions articles for mass and a copy of a bull of 1575 were found. Mayne and Tregian were taken to Launceston gaol, and more than twenty others were charged with various offences at the September assizes. But the affair of Mayne the priest was a test case, and great interest was aroused at the outcome of his trial.

Arraigned at Launceston, Mayne was declared guilty of treason, the jury having been directed to bring in this verdict by the senior of the judges present. Sentence, however, was referred to the Privy Council, on account of the other judges' dissatisfaction at the proceedings. Grenville went up to Court to see his desire was effected. The Council determined to make an example of Mayne, and sent down a warrant for his execution. The first of many seminary and regular priests who were to die under the penal laws against the Catholics, Mayne was hanged, drawn and quartered at Launceston on 29th November, 1577. By the Roman Church he is considered a martyr; his heroism and faith all would recognize. A portion of his skull, recovered at the time of his execution, is preserved as a precious relic at Lanherne, and a yearly pilgrimage at Launceston honours his memory.

The others implicated were dealt with in various ways. Tregian was condemned to loss of lands and liberty, and his house at Golden was broken into and despoiled. Years of imprisonment in the Fleet followed, till, his health giving way, he was allowed to live at Chelsea in the closing years of Elizabeth's reign. He died in Spain in 1608. The manors and lands passed out of the Tregian ownership into the hands of new, and safely protestant, families.

There were not a few among Cornishmen who were dissatisfied with the Elizabethan Church. Exeter College was well known for its Catholic sympathies, and many West country students went abroad to the seminary at Douai (it was transferred to Rheims from 1578 to 1593) to be prepared for the Roman priesthood. Two incumbents of Cornish parishes became disillusioned by the Anglican compromise, and went into exile for their newfound faith. Thomas Bluett, rector of St. Michael Penkevil, and John Vivian, rector of St. Just-in-Roseland, left the country and made for Allen's seminary. In due course both returned to the English mission. Later Bluett was imprisoned and vanishes from view. Vivian also was kept in prison for a while, but was sent out of the country in 1585.

There were several other students from Cornwall in the first years of Cardinal Allen's foundation. A poor lad from Bodmin, John Curry, and a yeoman of St. Wenn, John Tippet, were ordained in the year of Mayne's death, 1577; the latter died in exile. Daniel Kemp, a member of the recusant Kemps of St. Minver, arrived at the college in 1581, and another Kemp, Francis, in 1589. The story is told that Sir John Arundell passing a group of schoolboys at play, noticed another sitting by a hedge reading. He gave the lad a gold piece, became his patron, and sent him to Exeter College. After this, the young man, John Cornelius, went abroad to Rheims, on to Rome, and returning became chaplain to Sir John. In 1581 Cornelius had preached before the pope in the Sistine Chapel and his eloquence, there recognized, was such as to draw many to his Church. William Bawden, another Cornishman, was a pupil of Cornelius'.

Of lay Catholics of note there were not a few. Perhaps the most distinguished among Cornishmen was Nicholas Roscarrock. While in prison for the faith he compiled a register of British saints, in which are translations of the lives of Cornish saints as current at the Reformation.

With the development of European crisis and the plots against the queen the penal legislation was made more severe. The Act of 1581, which made it treason to reconcile or be reconciled to Rome also raised the fine for non-attendance at the Anglican service to £20 a month. This made it impossible for any but the richest Catholic families to survive unless they conformed to the established Church. Nevertheless, it seems that these laws, harsh though they were, were only partially and intermittently enforced in all their severity. Except in times of tension or after some rumour of a 'popish plot', real or pretended, wealthy or influential recusants might avoid the worst penalties and continue Catholic services in secret in their houses.

The closing years of Elizabeth's reign were complicated by a controversy within the ranks of the English Catholics and between the secular and regular clergy. It was thought possible that an oath recognizing the queen's supremacy could be framed, allowing the spiritual jurisdiction of the pope to be maintained. These efforts failed, however, and the government, taking advantage of the situation, fomented the dissention between the parties.

Sir John Arundell died in 1590, and his widow retired to Chideock in Dorset. The fortunes of the family were by this time depleted by the heavy fines, but loyalty to their faith remained. In 1594 Cornelius, who had been ministering to the household at Chideock, was discovered in hiding, tried at Dorchester on a charge of treason, condemned, and executed. The Cornish home at Lanherne, however, continued to keep alive the Catholic faith of the tenants, and priests came and went as heretofore. But by that time Cornish Catholicism was a small cause, worn down by fines, confiscations and imprisonments.

At the time of the Civil War the recusants in the county, as elsewhere, were devoted Royalists. They had more to hope for from a king sympathetic to their religion than from a Parliament bitterly opposed to prelacy and popery. There was a Parliamentarian accusation that Lanherne sheltered ten or more seminary priests in 1642, and that the Arundells were in the forefront of those raising forces for the king. As a young squire of nineteen John Arundell joined the king's forces at Boconnoc in 1644, and was knighted for his gallantry in the war. He was the last of that line to live in the old home at Lanherne, which after his death in 1701 was only occasionally inhabited and fell into disrepair, though in 1706 there was a priest there, named Martin Gifford. In time the house passed through marriage to the Wardour branch of the Arundell family.

A religious census in 1671 showed a small concentration of Catholics in the parishes of Cardinham, Treneglos, Mawgan, Newlyn and St. Ervan, totalling 67 in all; in addition, no doubt, children and servants should be added, but the Catholic remnant was on the wane. Registration of Catholic property was required from time to time, and in 1715 such an inquiry disclosed there was still a handful of recusants in the county, of whom the most wealthy was Richard Arundell. The names of those registered include the Rawes, Hannes, Pearces and others prominent in recusant history. In the returns made to the bishop of Exeter in 1767 there appear further names, Menna, Benny, Jolly, Bulger, Thomas Hanne, 'pretender to physic', and Richard Rawe, described as 'esquire'. It is plain that the Catholics were a scattered group, mostly humble folk in the region of the Arundell properties, and accepted by the majority as a permanent feature in Cornish life. They lived their withdrawn lives, from which the shadows lift from time to time to disclose their faithfulness in their religion. A member of the Hanne family, Charles, born in 1711 at Deviock became a Jesuit at twenty, and died in 1799. The Couche household at Torfrey, Golant, maintained a priest, Richard Hayman, also a Jesuit, who died there in 1756, and so on. The penal laws had fallen into abeyance, but some over-zealous magistrate might at any time stir up trouble, or mobs could rouse a 'No Popery' riot to harry the Catholics almost at will.

Toleration dawned in 1778, and from 1791 it was possible for mass to be said publicly. Understanding of the Catholics was greatly helped by the flood of *émigrés* from the French Revolution, including many priests and religious of both sexes. Moved by the plight of some English Carmelite nuns, turned out of their convent in Antwerp, Lord Arundell of Wardour made Lanherne available to them in 1794. Here they settled, and the growth of romanticism and toleration made the 'nunnery' a centre of interest. French priests, too, persuaded the prejudiced that they were normal people, and public sympathy gave them a welcome.

John Whitaker, rector of Ruan Lanyhorne, had correspondence with the Abbé Gordon, and dined with him when he came to Cornwall in 1793. The fascination of Rome grew. Sir Harry Trelawny, descendant of bishop Trelawny, having been successively dissenting minister, and Anglican vicar of Egloshayle, completed his pilgrimage by joining the Roman Church, and was ordained as a priest in Italy, where he died in 1834. His daughters – he was widowed when ordained – long maintained a priest at Trelawne.

The influx of Irish to Cornwall for mining and, later, new railway workings, and the immigration of German and Austrian refugees from political upheaval increased the Catholic population greatly. The mission at Falmouth, begun about 1805 in a private room, soon led to the building of a church, the congregation growing rapidly after the Catholic Emancipation Act of 1829. William Young, a priest at Lanherne, lectured at St. Columb in 1840 on the Roman Catholic faith in open meetings. Later that year he began the building of a church at Penzance, where the cause was lapsing after the removal of its first priest, William Ivers, in 1837. Then in 1846 Young began a mission at Bodmin. Altogether he deserves the title 'apostle of Cornwall' given him by his co-religionists. At Camborne there were 250 in the congregation, mostly Irish, in 1853.

The setting up of the new hierarchy in 1850, with a bishop at Plymouth facilitated the spread of Roman Catholicism and brought a new zeal which won many converts. At Bodmin, there is St. Mary's Abbey of the Canons Regular of the Lateran, whose clergy serve scattered local chapelries, and also prepare men for the priesthood. A few convents exist in Cornwall and engage in educational, hospital and other activities. Several churches of architectural merit have been erected, of which the most noteworthy is that at Launceston, dedicated to the English Martyrs.

II – Presbyterians and Congregationalists

The pastors who were ejected from their benefices in 1660–62 could not look for toleration if they continued their ministry elsewhere. The Restoration government soon took in hand a series of repressive measures directed against those who would not conform to the resettled Anglican position. Under the Conventicle Act of 1664 no religious service other than that of the Church of England was permitted except in private houses and in the presence of not more than five in addition to those of the household. The penalties for non-compliance were increased in 1670. The Corporation Act of 1661, and the Test Act of 1673 prohibited nonconformists from holding office in municipal or governmental affairs; the receiving of the Eucharist according to the rite of the Church of England was made the test for office.

Generally speaking nonconformity was illegal up to 1689, though in many parts meetings were connived at. The reason for the harsh treatment of dissenters was a dread of return to military rule, as experienced under the Commonwealth, and the fear of the establishment of Roman Catholicism. Under the Toleration Act of William and Mary, 1689, and later Acts, the meetingplaces of protestant dissenters could be licensed by the clerk of the peace for the county, or by the bishop of the diocese. Ministers also had to be licensed, and preachers of more suspiciously regarded sects sometimes found the authorities used the right of inspecting licences as a way of stopping services.

So far as Cornwall is concerned about fifty ministers were deprived of their livings by the Act of 1662; of these, many had been instituted during the Commonwealth when the previous, and Anglican, incumbent was put out as 'unsuitable' for the ministry. The nonconformist ministers in several cases endeavoured to carry on meetings in some secluded spot or remote farm, at considerable risk to themselves and their flocks. In some cases the ministers lived quietly, attended the parish church and scraped a livelihood from their own property, or by working in some humble employment.

William White resided at Michell after ejectment from Ladock and 'behaveth himself with much and due reverence' in the services at Newlyn in 1665. Nathanael Tingcombe, ejected out of the parish of Lansallos, lived peaceably at Fowey on his 'temporal estate', and at St. Michael Penkevil Joseph Halsey, put out of the living, was allowed to rent the parsonage from the Anglican incumbent. All this was reported by the rural deans in accordance with regulations for keeping a strict watch on nonconformists in 1665.

But others were not content to live peaceably under a regime of which they could not conscientiously approve. Thomas Tregoss, onetime curate at St. Ives and ejected vicar of Mylor and Mabe, continued to hold his meetings in the parish of Budock. For persisting in his ministry he was imprisoned several times and fined £200. It is evident his ministrations were popular. John Collyer, vicar of Budock and St. Gluvias wrote in 1670 to Francis Cooke and explains that one reason for the frequentation of Tregoss's meetings is that there is no 'sermon at Gluvias Sundays in the afternoon. Every forenoon (as I am informed) I have the greatest part of them, but when I go to Budock in the afternoon many of them frequent Tregoss'. Meetings continued, and established themselves at Treliever in Mabe parish, and at Falmouth. William Olver ministered at Launceston, sustained by a pension from 'Mr Secretary Morice' and his Mastership of the Grammar School. By

1718 as many as 130 hearers were attached to the meeting which became an Independent cause.

Joseph Sherwood gathered a considerable following at Penzance after his eviction from St. Hilary, and also laboured at St. Ives and Marazion, laying the foundations of evangelical effort which in the first town has continued to this day. The former vicar of Wendron and Helston 'the old Mr. Jagoe, the grand nonconformist of these parts and a great Conventicler' preached and took service at Helston church without licence or conformity; 'he adds to and diminishes the service at his pleasure' in spite of the wrath of the bishop's official, Jasper Phillips, and local justices. He had much popular support.

At Saltash there were no less than six ministers living, Messrs. Toms, Tyack, Hicks, Vine, Lydstone and Travers, who were suspected of carrying on conventicles in the town and district. Altogether, it seems there were a number of small causes in the county, changing their place of meeting, and coalescing and separating in a most confusing way as circumstances and opening compelled. One such of more than passing interest was at Gunrounson in St. Enoder parish. Here a dissenting cause was established by Henry Flamank, the 'outed' minister of Lanivet. He was licensed, in the first move towards recognition of dissent, in 1672, and continued to minister at the meeting, in a farmhouse, till 1697 or thereabout. Afterwards his elder brother Roger, once vicar of Sithney, took over. It was a small meeting, and in frequent receipt of financial help from the Exeter Assembly.

This Assembly was a renewal of the association in the west of Presbyterian congregations between 1655–59. Voluntary associations of ministers and congregations were again set up after the Toleration Act of 1689, and attempts were made to regulate such matters as training and ordination of candidates, a union of Presbyterian and Independent ministries and congregations and so forth. The

Exeter Assembly *Minutes* 1691–1717 throw a considerable light on the nonconformist history of Cornwall at the beginning of the eighteenth century.

There were several Cornish meetings which, from time to time, needed help from the fund supported by the more prosperous congregations. Gunrounson is frequently mentioned as in receipt of aid for the support of its minister. After Roger Flamank's death in 1708, James Strong was sent to succeed him in 1709 and was ordained at Bodmin in 1710. Towards the end of his ministry at Gunrounson – he left in 1717 – he was tending, as many of his ministerial brethren then were, towards Arianism in theology. Some of his congregation, who lived at Grampound, grew dissatisfied and set up a Baptist meeting at Grampound under the care of John Burford and linked it with Penryn (1738).

In 1717 the Assembly had a complaint from Bodmin that their minister, John Greby, was not ordained and that the congregation was indifferent to that fact. They suggested he should be ordained before the end of the year. To Liskeard went a commission to look into the case of Richard Glanvill; it suspended him for immorality (to which he confessed) and after penance restored him to his office. Jasper Howe of Penryn wished to know if the meeting at that town should be joined with the one at Falmouth? The Assembly continued as a source of encouragement, advice, and order as well as of financial help till about 1753.

With the growth of toleration and the dawn of the 'Age of Reason' the points for which the old dissenters stood seemed to be less vital. In the reaction from the hard Calvinism of their fathers of Commonwealth days many Presbyterian ministers adopted Arian views. There was great controversy in the Assemblies of 1717–20. Many meetings became Arianized, some languished and died, some became Independent or Baptist.

Replies to the bishop's questions in 1744 reveal the then state of dissent. They are illuminating. There were Presbyterian meetinghouses at Liskeard and St. Martin-by-Looe, and one at Bodmin with only six or seven families supporting it. At Fowey the meetinghouse had no minister and there were but five families of that faith. The two Presbyterian families at Marazion attended the church there rather than their own meeting in Penzance. The rector of Creed, John Hughes, reports that there were five or six persons 'Anabaptists', who were formerly more numerous, with a poor dwellinghouse to meet in – 'their teacher is one Buffet of Penryn who now seldom visits 'em, to so low a condition, by ye Blessing of God, are they reduced'.

John Hughes, however, lived to see a fresh wind of evangelical zeal blow through the cold theology of the older dissent. That had retained much of the strain of Calvinism and the starkness of Puritanism in its ethos. It continued the grave unliturgical services of the Commonwealth time, the infrequent but earnestly prepared communions, the strictly ordered living and the sombre attire.

The Evangelical Revival developed eventually, as we have seen, several wings. Anglican clergy of that school of thought largely embraced the Calvinistic theology which they saw in the Thirty-nine Articles. The Methodists who followed Wesley were Arminians, and in time an antipathy developed between them and Calvinists, especially after 1770 when the controversy reached its climax. The 'Methodists' who associated themselves with George Whitfield and Lady Huntingdon, however, were Calvinists in doctrine and to them the older dissenters felt affinity. With the renewed emphasis everywhere on the 'warmed heart' the older congregations benefited, and fresh life flowed in the old channels, though some features of dissent did not survive.

After the death of Samuel Walker, the

universally-respected curate of Truro in 1761, the ministry at St. Mary's was continued by Charles Pye, a Latitudinarian of flippant speech who was unacceptable to Walker's converts. Some of these seceded and set up a dissenting cause in the town, which absorbed the remnants of the older Presbyterian meeting. Through their occupancy of the old cockpit as their place of meeting the supporters of the infant cause became known as 'Cockpittarians' till their new chapel was built in 1776.

Another dissenting cause has its interest, in that it was formed at Looe by Sir Harry Trelawny. Influenced at Oxford and adopting the tenets of dissent, he preached in his home district and formed a congregation at Looe. In 1777 he was ordained at Southampton as pastor of the Looe church. His views underwent changes, and in 1781 he was made deacon and ordained priest by bishop Ross at Exeter, became vicar of St. Allen and then of Egloshayle, and finally was admitted into the Roman Church, being ordained as priest by Cardinal Odescalchi; he died in Italy in 1834.

The renewed prosperity of the nonconformist causes led to the formation of many village meetings, on the basis of Independency with a Calvinistic theology. In 1802 the Cornwall Association of Congregational Churches was formed at Tregony to promote fraternal relationships between the Independent groups in the county. By 1821 there were thirty-three churches of this polity in Cornwall, from Launceston to Penzance.

Remaining disabilities of the dissenters were removed in the course of the nineteenth century, nonconformists being admitted to the Universities in 1854–71, and by 1880 Free Church ministers were empowered to officiate in consecrated ground in cemeteries.

The denominational history of the rest of the nineteenth century must be passed over rapidly, merely recording outstanding trends. It would seem that the old Calvinism gave way to a more tolerant theology, and that the earlier evangelical fervour passed over into zeal for the matters then in public debate – education, with a struggle from c.1830–1902 with the Church of England, temperance, Ireland, disestablishment of the Church, and Sunday work. Bitter strife over the Education Acts of 1870 and 1902 rallied the nonconformist Churches to the Liberal party, which many had long supported. Chapel pulpits became the platform for political opinions expressed with ardour and sincerity.

Since then the return to the spiritual nature of the Christian witness has been noteworthy. The old bitternesses have largely gone with successive moves towards understanding between the Free Churches and Anglicanism, and the growth of apathy towards religion generally. Decline of village causes, and economic factors, have however reduced the Congregational churches in Cornwall to less than a score.

III – The Baptists

The Commonwealth period was one given to much discussion about religious polity, but it manifested little spirituality. By way of reaction men sought refreshment in new directions, and groups with Baptist views emerged.

Most probably these opinions were first propagated in Cornwall by soldiers in Cromwell's New Model Army, the officers of which were not uncommonly Baptists. Certainly the daughter of George Kekewich, governor of St. Mawes Castle, was baptized in the sea about 1650. The names of John Pendarves, John Carew and Hugh Courtney are mentioned as those of prominent Baptists at the time, and the Baptist preacher Anna Trapnel tried to visit Courtney when he was imprisoned. After this, preaching at Bodmin and public baptisms initiated Baptist work farther east, and there was soon (1656) a meeting at Looe of baptized believers.

Thomas Tregoss, the 'outed' vicar of Mylor, who was the founder of dissenting congregations in the Penryn–Falmouth area, seems also to have originated Baptist congregations there, though it is not clear if he himself held those views. There was a Baptist society at Falmouth between 1663 and 1671, the cause also being settled at Treliever.

The Baptists became perforce dissenters after the settlement of 1662. Their conception of the Church as a gathered and confessing community could not be reconciled with the idea, accepted by Presbyterian and Anglican alike, that the nation and the Church were one. The Exeter Assembly did not include Baptists, and they made their lonely way through the eighteenth century with small groups in the towns and surrounding villages.

John Burford was the minister at Treliever for a while from 1722, and moved the meeting to Penryn about 1728. The Grampound Baptists were linked to this about ten years later. After Burford's departure in 1741 there was a decline, until in 1764 a revival of Baptist life came about with the opening of a meeting at Chacewater. This meeting originated from the interest of the Hornblowers, who came to Chacewater as engineers, being already convinced Baptists. The little congregation was helped by visitors from Plymouth and public preaching commenced in 1767. As a result the Falmouth congregation came together again and the two causes were worked as one.

Periods of prosperity and of difficulty followed. James Bicheno, a forward-looking man, ministered from 1778–80. His outlook was broad, admitting non-Baptists to communion and allowing women the vote at church meetings. His successor was Samuel Wildbore, an unprepossessing man who was not a Baptist, but an Independent who did not declare his views until later, when he took several members with him over to the Independents! A renewal of the link with Chacewater came with the ministry of Robert Redding, whose views were stricter; he excluded all but baptized believers from communion. This rigidity did not continue.

Redding, who later ministered at Truro (1790–1807), was the father of Cyrus Redding, the voluminous writer of books, poems, and articles on a variety of matters other than religious. Cyrus launched, on behalf of the Parliamentary Reformers, the first issue of the *West Briton* newspaper in July 1810.

A considerable activity among Baptists at the close of the eighteenth century and opening decades of the nineteenth gave them a prosperity in numbers. The incumbents' Returns of 1821 show there were several little meetings of Baptists in Cornish parishes. Those at Creed used the same meetinghouse as the Congregationalists. At St. Erth there was a Calvinist room, used by Baptists, Presbyterians, and Congregationalists, who all shared those views.

The Falmouth Baptists formed a strong centre. They collected £17 for the widows and orphans of Trafalgar in 1805. They set six young men to work evangelising the country villages round about. Later on, newcomers to the congregation, the Freemans, began local work for the Y.M.C.A. An interesting fact is that the first wedding in a dissenting chapel in Falmouth after the legislation permitting it was passed, took place in 1838 at the chapel of the Baptists.

The zeal of Baptist converts outran discretion on occasion. In 1824 John Jeffrey, a convert of George C. Smith, minister of the Penzance Baptists, wrote adverse comments on the state of religion in the district which seemed to reflect on the Methodists. A paper war ensued, known as the 'Tucknet' controversy, from an illustration used by one of the warriors of the pen.

Smith was a converted sailor, and became pastor of the Penzance Baptists, 1807–25, 1848–63, building six chapels in neighbouring villages. He was the founder of several sailors' hostels, and became known in consequence as the 'Sailors' Friend'.

The wave of prosperity for the Baptists in the early nineteenth century, however, declined and drew back. Many village chapels closed, and only a few causes flourished. The Falmouth church retained, and retains, its vigour in spite of the erosion of the years. It has been served by ministers of distinction in the denomination and in the field of scholarship, such as William Burchell, 1824–39; Fuller Gooch, 1872–78, and Venis Robinson, 1908–16; this last was father of Theodore, writer of standard works on Semitic culture.

Successively removed to Market Street in 1877 and to its present site in 1939, the Falmouth Baptist church remains the chief centre of work of that denomination in Cornwall.

IV – The Quakers

Another community arising in the period of the Commonwealth is the group known as Quakers. Their founder, George Fox, turned away from the religious professors of his day to find an 'inner light' as his guide. His views derived in part from the Baptists. Fox was in Cornwall in 1655 with some friends and as a result of his publishing a manifesto in West Cornwall was imprisoned after sentence by Justice Glyn for thirty weeks in the noisome gaol at Launceston.

Much sympathy and curiosity resulted. Fox was visited by a widow, Loveday Hambly of Tregongeeves near St. Austell. Her farm became a hub from which Quakerism expanded to every part of the county. Another disciple was Thomas Mounce of Liskeard, and on this man's farm many general meetings of the Quakers were held.

The Quakers, or 'Friends' as they preferred to be

known, quickly aroused opposition and brought on themselves much trouble. Their refusal to swear an oath, holding that such was forbidden in Scripture, brought them into collision with the secular authorities. They also refused to pay tithes, or church rates for the repair of what they called the 'steeplehouse' or 'the pope's old decayed masshouse'. Neither would they take off their hats out of respect, or bear arms. For these things they were the victims of distraint, and imprisonment. Many Friends were imprisoned more than once. Loveday Hambly herself went to Bodmin prison for several weeks, and had her household and farm goods distrained for not paying rates. In 1657 Thomas Mounce had a cow taken from him. Edmund Hinks was sentenced to prison for speaking to the 'priest' of Truro, John Tingcombe, in the service there; he was however permitted to remain at his home because his children might have had to be maintained by the parish. Mounce was presented by the Liskeard churchwardens in 1665 for 'causing a burial place to be built on his land'. The names Lower, Deeble, Upcott, Tregelles and others constantly appear in the accounts of the Cornish Quakers' 'Sufferings'.

From 1675 to 1700 the Friends made rapid headway, and meetinghouses sprang up after the Toleration Act of 1689. By 1700 there were 27 societies in the county with about 400 adherents.

Within a few decades there was a considerable decline. The Visitation returns show that in many parishes the numbers had shrunk. In St. Endellion the meetinghouse in 1765 was 'seldom frequented', and the same is reported of the parishes of St. Minver and St. Stephen-in-Brannel.

The Quaker community, largely composed of middle class folk, became an inward-looking group. The influence they wielded however has always been out of proportion to numbers. Almost exceptional in prominence was the Fox family namesakes of the founder of Quakerism

– at Falmouth. Rich, generous, with wide connections through shipping and consular service, the family became as it were protectors of Cornish Quakerism.

There are meetinghouses of Friends in Cornwall, but they are few and retired. The most attractive is undoubtedly that near Feock, erected about 1710, a thatched room with the lovely name of Come-to-Good.

V – Later Methodism

The death of John Wesley in 1791 was for many Methodists the removal of the last link which bound them to the Church of England, and the fall of the cornerstone holding the Methodist system together. The strong affection they had for their spiritual father – they did not hesitate to use that very title for their beloved leader – was a personal thing which could not be transferred to another and still less to a corporate body such as the Conference, however venerable that institution may have seemed to them to be. Many questions closed during Wesley's lifetime were now seen to be open again. What was to be the future relation with the Anglican Church? What authority remained in Conference, with each preacher? What was the relationship between preacher and members?

There were already ideas of reform in the air, ultra-democratic suggestions as to the government of the Connexion were mooted. In the towns particularly there was a strong desire on the part of the societies for complete sacramental independence, and in many quarters a loss of early zeal which roused the ire of earnest souls. All this gave rise to incompatible blocks of opinion within the Methodist body which issued in a melancholy series of divisions and offshoots in the half century following Wesley's death.

In June 1791 a radical manifesto appeared proposing widespread modifications of Methodist polity, signed by many Redruth Methodists among them Dr. Boase, a prominent apothecary in the town, which was sent to every travelling preacher in the kingdom. Had these proposals found implementation, Methodism would have been reduced to a series of independent congregations. It is evident that in Redruth there was much dissatisfaction with the old ways, and it causes no surprise that the first secession from Methodism in Cornwall took place in that town with the resignation of some ninety members who followed Boase in September 1802 in forming a separate society. They erected a chapel of their own and opened preaching in other places.

Another small schism took place at Truro, led by John Boyle, at about the same time as Dr. Boase's people seceded at Redruth.

Elsewhere in the country of course other groups were forming with a revised organization, such as the Methodist New Connexion. But doctrinally there were no points at issue with the old and larger part of the Methodist body.

By the turn of the century successive Conferences had worked out the problem of sacramental administration and set out the 'Plan of Pacification' in 1795. Any society which by a majority of the members wished for service in 'church hours' or the sacraments to be administered by the preachers could seek permission from the Conference. This satisfied the many who openly wished to be self-sufficient, and at the same time preserved the continuance in the Church of England ordinances for those of the 'old plan' who desired them. The Cornish societies at Launceston, Redruth, Gwennap, Helston and St. Ives were early in their acceptance of this Plan. Others followed suit so that in time it was usual in most larger societies for the sacraments to be administered in the chapel by the preachers.

In country districts, however, the 'old plan' long survived, the members of the Methodist society often being among the most regular attendants at the parish communion and at morning service. At places such as

Altarnun, Manaccan, Ruan Lanyhorne, St. Minver, St. Samson, Stoke Climsland, Colan, Cubert, St. Ewe, St. Wenn, Blisland, and many others the larger part of the society usually attended church in the morning in 1821, as the incumbents note in their replies of that year to the bishop. By 1833 the church connexions had greatly weakened, except for a lingering sentiment for the sacraments at the parish church, which still obtains in some districts.

In spite of the divisions and tensions which distracted Methodism, its spiritual progress was not without incident. The great revivals which gave massive numbers to the Connexion still continued, especially in West Cornwall. The years 1799, 1814 and 1831 were years of intense fervour, principally in the mining parishes of the west. Here mining and Methodism took on that close identification which is obvious in the juxtaposition of old mine workings and Methodist chapels.

The first reliable returns of numbers duly admitted into the societies date from 1767, when Cornish Methodists numbered 2,160. In 1790 the total was about 4,000. In 1830 it had risen to 16,691. In many villages, it was claimed, over ninety per cent of the population attended ministrations, either as hearers or as full members; Methodism was, it has been said, the 'established church' of Cornwall.

Its followers were won in barns, in mines, in chapels, and not in the parish churches, and around these humbler shrines their affections naturally grew.

The 'Great Revival' of 1814 broke out at a love feast at Camborne on Sunday, 6th February. A young man named Henry Andrew Vivian was present and has left a diary of the stirring times which followed. Unparalleled scenes were witnessed, the chapel at Tuckingmill for instance being 'occupied without intermission both day and night' for nearly a whole week. Again large increases in almost every society in the district were reported. It had to be admitted, however that there was often a considerable falling-away afterwards, and that the excitement of revivals often produced results tragic and sordid in the less stable of the hearers.

The strong concentration of Methodism in the west will have been noticed. By contrast the eastern part of the county had not had the constant attention of Wesley and his helpers, and the societies were small and scattered. This riveted the attention of William Brian (who adopted as an adult the spelling of his name as O'Bryan), an earnest young man of Luxulyan, who in zeal for souls went preaching round the parishes of north Cornwall, forming societies which he faithfully joined into the Wesleyan denomination. But this work clashed with his duties as a local preacher among the Methodists, and he was peremptorily expelled from that body, the ruling being made public in the very chapel at Gunwen for which he had given the land.

O'Bryan then began the formation of a separate Connexion and was working within a short time in north Cornwall and north Devon with great success. From 1815 his work was wholly distinct from the older Wesleyanism. The Bryanites, or as they called themselves, 'Bible Christians', were characterized by a mysticism almost Quaker-like, with emotional preaching and a Celtic reliance on signs and dreams.

The Thornes of Shebbear in north Devon threw in their lot with O'Bryan, and James Thorne was invited to travel as the second itinerant in 1816. By this time there were 237 members. Female preachers were allowed and appointed. By 1817 the preaching had spread to the villages round Truro, where Boyle's society joined them, St. Neot, Kilkhampton, and Shebbear. At this last place the first chapel of the new Connexion was built in 1817. It was the original practice of the Bible Christians to avoid those places where there was a Methodist society already established. As time went on, however, O'Bryan and his helpers considered themselves free to go where opportunity presented itself. This angered many Wesleyan people, as they saw their 'rights' infringed, just as in the previous century the parish clergy had been provoked by the original Methodist mission. Thus began that feature of many Cornish villages – rival chapels within a stone's throw, competing for the attention of a handful of people, and providing headaches for modern Methodist administrators. O'Bryan himself broke away from his own organization in 1829, went to America, and died in New York in 1868.

The Wesleyan Methodist Association was another offshoot which became strong in parts of Cornwall. The immediate occasion of this Connexional split, which gravely affected Cornwall, was the proposal to establish a 'Theological Institution'. This met with opposition by reason of fears of stereotyping ministerial training, jealousy of the nominated president, Dr. Jabez Bunting, and resentment at the unconstitutional haste with which the scheme was pushed through. Dr. Samuel Warren violently attacked the proposal, and after trial at a special district meeting was suspended from his office as preacher. His cause was eagerly taken up. Warren travelled the country in support of reforms which he was advocating, and in Cornwall much sympathy was shown.

The Camelford quarterly meeting in the last weeks of 1834 was the scene of the opening of the dispute in Cornwall. Thomas Pope Rosevear, one of the most influential laymen in the county, and a forceful character, was put out of membership of the Methodist society for his advocacy of reform. The majority of the members – 634 out of 702 – nearly all the local preachers, with almost all the chapels and the societies at St. Tudy, St. Teath, Tintagel, Treligga, Forrabury and Minster became as a consequence the nucleus of the local Wesleyan Methodist Association.

In 1835 about forty members of the Polperro society

turned over to the Association and in Polruan too many joined the new denomination. Helston was another place where the Wesleyan Methodist Association had an early origin, a large proportion of the older society going over. At Liskeard services were held in the market hall until 1837, when a chapel was commenced. The Wesleyan Methodist Association continued in being until 1857, when amalgamation with the Wesleyan Reformers took place.

Another secession in west Cornwall occurred in favour of teetotalism. Many had become convinced that there was no alternative to total abstinence as a result of the great increase in drunkenness in the 1830s. James Teare spoke at two meetings in St. Ives Wesleyan chapel in 1838 advocating total abstinence, and formed a local temperance society. In a few years the membership at St. Ives was said to be 2,810 out of a population of about 5,000. This progress was paralleled all over Cornwall, many Methodists supporting the cause. But many preachers among the Methodists were not abstainers; Wesley had only discouraged the drinking of spirits, and in many chapel vestries there was a bottle for the preacher.

The holding of temperance meetings on chapel premises was eventually forbidden by the Wesleyan Conference of 1841, and the use of unfermented grape juice for the sacrament was not allowed. Later in that year about 250 teetotallers broke away from the St. Ives society, with another 150 from the village societies round about. A 'Teetotal Wesleyan Methodist' body came into being and a circuit was set up with about twenty-four preachers. But the denomination, which was confined to west Cornwall, had only a short life and by 1865 most of its members had merged with other offshoots from the Methodist body. Its witness, however, had had its effect and the principles of teetotalism were eventually adopted by the Wesleyan Conference itself.

Another upheaval, perhaps the greatest of all,

occurred in 1849. Three ministers, one of them a Cornishman, Samuel Dunn, born at Mevagissey in 1798, had been expelled from the Wesleyan ministry, as a result of the *Fly Sheet* controversy; these were letters advocating further reforms in Methodism. The whole Connexion was stirred, and in the five years following something like a hundred thousand members were lost to the Wesleyan body. In the autumn of 1851 reform meetings were held in many places in Cornwall, chapels of the New Connexion, Primitive Methodists, the Association, and the Baptists being loaned for the purpose. Dunn himself came to Camborne in 1850, where some years previously he had been a minister, and at the meeting in the open air at which he spoke it was estimated that ten thousand were present!

The course of the Reformers was similar to those of other secessions – after a continuance for a time they coalesced with some other group of similar views. In 1857 the 'United Methodist Free Churches' came into being, absorbing many who had been cast adrift by the nationwide travails of Methodism, which had resulted in rivalries and competition embittering the life of village and town.

The history of later Methodism is not all strife, however. Faithfulness to the record requires the unhappy tale of division to be recounted; it was the reflection in Methodism of the great wave of desire for reform in nation and in Europe. But there was another side to Methodist life, and to this we turn with relief. There was a selflessness in supporting the chosen cause and of this we find examples in every branch of Cornish Methodism. Devotion was nurtured by the Wesleys' hymns, which also formed a 'body of divinity' available to all. Methodism remained throughout the early nineteenth century a revivalist body; the high sacramentalism of the founders and of the first years of Methodism was not typical later, certainly in Cornwall.

Among Methodist worthies 'Billy Bray' a miner of Twelveheads near Truro, stands pre-eminent. His preaching on behalf of the Bible Christians has become a legend in the county. He tramped long distances after a hard day's work to fulfil preaching engagements, and in his spare time built with his own hands chapels for his Connexion. For forty years his little nimble figure moved about Cornwall, preaching, praying, shouting, eager for the cause of the Gospel and of teetotalism.

Heroic in a different way was Michael Verran, a Methodist miner of Callington. At work in 1842 on a shaft with two companions, he was preparing a charge to loosen the rock, one comrade having gone to the surface to wind up the last two in turn. The fuse became ignited too soon, and Verran offered to remain below to give his friend a chance of quick escape at the risk of a terrible death. The explosion blew stones to the top of the shaft, but Verran was found only bruised, sheltered by a piece of plank and the strength of his prayers. Reports of this incident came to the ears of Thomas Carlyle, a subscription list was opened and Verran received some rudiments of education.

It is with the remembrance of this sort of religious fervour, mystical, emotional, devoted, thoroughly Celtic that we must look at many of the humbler places of worship which grace our moors and smaller villages. They have a story which is more worth treasuring than that of the sometimes pretentious buildings of a later and more comfortable Methodism.

The older Wesleyanism still carried with it a flavour of Anglicanism. The Plan of Pacification had laid it down in 1795 that when service was performed on Sundays in church hours the liturgy of the Prayer book should be used, or Wesley's abridgment of it, or at least the lessons in the calendar. The Prayer book was a familiar part of Methodist worship, particularly at the morning service, though not so common in Cornwall as elsewhere. By the 1840s, however, the rise of 'Ritualism' in the Church of England, with the appeal to the Prayer book as capable of, nay, requiring, a Catholic interpretation 'set the popish cat among the Wesleyan pigeons'. From then on the Anglican liturgy became the object of suspicion, and many chapels ceased to use it.

In 1874 the Wesleyan Conference was held at Camborne, and a proposal was made that a revision of the whole liturgy should be undertaken, removing expressions which gave offence to evangelical protestants. These principally related to absolution by the priest, baptismal regeneration, and so forth. A vocal minority pressed for the total abolition of any liturgy. However the motion was carried, and nine years later a *Book of Public Prayers and Offices* was produced and adopted, being a liturgy marking the protestantism and ecclesiastical independence of Methodism. With union in 1932, of course, further revision has taken place.

The later years of the nineteenth century saw a great 'Forward Movement', and the desire for closer union between the many fragments of the Methodist body. The recession in mining in the latter half of the nineteenth century however set back the Methodist cause in the county through the emigration of many devoted members, but the flavour of Cornish Methodism penetrated many parts of the wider Methodist communion overseas as a consequence.

Among the many influences making attractive the faith of Methodists was the writing of Mark Guy Pearse, a Cornishman born at Camborne in 1842, who became a preacher among the Wesleyans and a writer of distinction. His *Daniel Quorm and His Religious Notions* (1874) was a popular book and won the approbation of bishop Benson, who called it 'admirable'. Many articles and pamphlets from his pen appeared in support of Methodist beliefs, and some are still read.

The fading of old animosities, and the growing belief that disunity did no credit to Christianity led to the amalgamation of some small branches of Methodism in 1907, when the Bible Christians merged with others of liberal views to form the United Methodist Church. The forming in 1896 of the 'Free Church Council' brought the nonconforming communions together, and the experiences of wartime, and the resulting economic difficulties, helped to promote further union in 1932, when all the strands of Methodism in this country were brought together in one Methodist Church. It is true to say however that there still survives the older outlook of the different branches which makes working together far from simple. One result of union has been the appointment of 'separated chairmen' of the districts, relieved of immediate circuit cares. In this new departure the Cornish district was one of the earliest to share.

Methodism today has practically discarded revivalism, though concern for evangelism is strong. The social and political implications of the Gospel have long been a concern of the Methodist people generally, and this interest continues in the united Church. The old discipline of the 'class' has died out, though here and there a modified system survives. Details of organization do not excite Methodists as they did at the time of the secessions; interest tends to be in persons, rather than in principles.

In the decades since the second war there has emerged a new valuation of pastoral work and a noticeable revival of emphasis on the sacraments, which is bearing fruit in more frequent and reverent administration of baptism and the Lord's Supper. This is important in view of the discussions on unity with the Church of England which have been a feature of the post-war years, since the gap between the two communions has been markedly closed by this and other trends, and prospects of unity are brighter than at any time in the past.

The problem of redundancy in a county like Cornwall, which has an overplus of chapels is being boldly tackled and in one or two areas new churches replace old buildings inadequate or ruinous. An attractive church of modern design may be seen at Trevellas, near St. Agnes.

Also of interest is the growing study of Methodist history in the county and the formation of the Cornish Methodist Historical Association to further this research into Methodist origins. And worthy of mention is the acquisition in 1949 of the old cottage at Trewint, near Altarnun, once the home of the Isbells, Wesley's hosts, where a 'shrine' has been formed which yearly attracts large numbers.

The strength of Methodism in Cornwall today can be gauged by the fact that in the Cornwall District (which does not quite coincide with the county, some eastern fringe areas being included in the Plymouth and Exeter District) there were in 1962 some 21,271 duly admitted members, ministered to by 77 Methodist ministers (not including supernumeraries) and a host of local preachers. In the same year the number of baptisms was 1,076. There are in the District two Methodist schools, the West Cornwall School and Truro School both of which have a high reputation for education of a grammar and public school kind.

Modern Methodism has a polity so delicately balanced as a result of the struggles of a hundred years ago that the proposals for unity with the Church of England, which involve the 'taking of episcopacy' into the Methodist system, will be viewed by many, at least in the county of Cornwall, as inviting a renewal of those fissiparous tendencies which so gravely weakened the witness of Wesley's disciples in the decades following his death.

6

Anglican Revival

THE COMMENCEMENT OF THE GREAT ANGLICAN RENEWAL IS
commonly dated from Keble's Assize sermon in 1833 at
Oxford on 'National Apostacy'. Thus the new stirring
practically coincided in the diocese of Exeter with the
opening of the episcopate of the redoubtable Henry
Phillpotts, who became bishop in 1831. But, as has already
been made clear, there was at least in Cornwall a good deal
of soil fruitfully prepared for propagating the rediscovered
truths, and indeed Phillpotts himself was a man of the old
scholarly high church kind.

The vast unwieldy diocese, with its large
concentration of population in the mining west, needed a
strong and fearless man at the head to effect needed reform
and recover the ground gained by an aggressive, successful
Methodism. Phillpotts was such a man, firm, strict, but
hardly endearing, being ready to invoke the law against
offenders on little provocation.

One of his first acts was to tour the whole diocese in
1831 in order to acquaint himself with the clergy and
leading laity. In the diary of the tour are many comments
on the clergy of the time, showing a shrewd judgement of
character and swift appraisal of a situation. He called on
Mr. Hoblyn, vicar of Mylor, and enters the comment 'ruled
by his wife?'. At St. Anthony-in-Roseland the church was

'ancient, small, and bad'. On 25th May he dined at Mawnan with Canon Rogers to meet a Clerical Club there. Veryan had Mr. Trist, youngish, 'said to be evangelical', and 'attentive to parish, especially Schools'. Dr. Hingston told him that St. Ives church – 'very handsome' – was 'almost deserted'. At St. Buryan he 'resolved to call on Mr. Stanhope (the dean) to provide a residence for a married curate in Sennen and St. Levan'.

On the basis of all this carefully gathered information the bishop prepared for his formal Visitation in 1833. The effect of his leadership was soon evident. From the 89 incumbents who resided on their cures in 1830 the number speedily rose, so that by the end of Phillpotts' episcopate there were 211 resident clergy and only six not living in their parishes and doing no duty there. The number of serving clergy rose from 191 to 271 in 1869. The building of new churches to serve the increased population in some Cornish parishes was also a care of the bishop. From 1830 to 1869 – the year of Phillpotts' death – more than 30 new churches were erected. Some of these were of little architectural merit and of poor material, giving the present generation many a problem. One or two have features of interest, in the story of their building rather than in the structures themselves.

The church at Baldhu was designed by William Haslam, who gained some reputation at the time for his ideas on church architecture. It was designed to serve a new mining population which in fact never materialized, so that the church today is remote and alone. The building is in a painfully correct Victorian version of a thirteenth century fabric, showing the result of the researches of the ecclesiological enthusiasts of the time. Haslam was then a 'Puseyite', a follower of the new Tractarian ideas, so that when bishop Phillpotts came to consecrate the church in 1848 there was a surpliced choir, a triptych behind the altar, candles, an organ, painted windows, and the service was chanted. This was unusual in the ordinary parish churches of the time.

Pendeen, on the bleak coast near St. Just, has a sturdier story, in that Robert Aitken, appointed the first vicar of this new parish, was a man of great spiritual power and moving eloquence. His faith was deeply evangelical, yet he had a conviction that perfection could only be reached by the sacraments. Many converts owed their spiritual awakening to him, some of the most eminent Roman Catholics of the time expressed their debt to him, and others became Anglican clergy or ministers in the Free Churches. He got the miners of the parish together to erect a temporary church, holding five hundred, which was soon packed every night. While they prayed they laboured, and soon a church, modelled on Iona Abbey in severe Early English style arose on that windy height, the cost of which was but that of sharpening the tools! Aitken was architect and clerk of works, the miners shaped the rocks to templates he cut out of newspaper and stuck to the boulders.

At the centre of the Church revival was the proclamation of the Catholic and traditional nature of the Church of England, truths which had seemed to be overlaid with the personal emphasis of the evangelicals, or the fact of 'establishment' and State control. The *Tracts for the Times* found many readers in Cornwall, and the expression of these ideas by the enrichment of the services was not slow to follow. There were already, as has been said, conscientious clergy who honoured the sacraments – Shuttleworth of St. Mary's, Penzance; Hobhouse, of St. Ive; Tatham, of Boconnoc; Hedgeland, who followed Shuttleworth at Penzance, and Kinsman of Tintagel, for instance. But the older men of the high church school, while rejoicing that their views so long in the shade were now aired on all sides, had not customarily innovated on the usual services beyond giving them an extra sincerity and decency. Now, all things were to be changed.

The idea that the parish church should be a small version of the cathedral with the choir chanting the service in the chancel immediately became popular. It was first found at the chapelry of Tregaminion, in the parish of Tywardreath. The ministry of Charles Lyne, and of his curate George Rundle Prynne, who afterwards became the heroic incumbent of St. Peter's, Plymouth, was of a Tractarian sort and the new chanted service was begun in 1843.

In the following year complaints against Walter Blunt, curate of Helston, led to a commission being appointed by the bishop to look into the matter. The churchwarden brought several charges against the curate – he wore the surplice in the pulpit instead of changing into his gown as was then usual. He did not pray before the sermon. He compelled all to remain on sacrament Sundays till the end of the exhortation. He would not bury anyone baptized by a dissenting minister, and so forth. Phillpotts (who had issued an order that surplices should be worn in preaching) finally judged Blunt to be in the right. On the matter of the surplice he wrote that it must be worn, because the vestments were not provided. If the parish provided the alb, vestment and cope 'I shall enjoin the minister, be he who he may, to use them'. William Coope, instituted rector of Falmouth in 1838 when he was only twenty-eight, got into trouble with his parishioners for his support of the Oxford Movement. His altar was furnished with lights in 1851, and his vestments, the first probably to be used in Cornwall in the Revival, survived until quite recently. Coope also wrote a series of *Falmouth Tracts* in which he set out the Catholic standpoint.

Robert Stephen Hawker, vicar of Morwenstow, the most northerly parish in the county, held the views of the old high church school tinged with Tractarianism. He commonly vested himself at service time in a white alb, and a chasuble, green on one side and amber on the other. This garb excited the admiration of Haslam in his 'Puseyite' stage, as did the bluff vicar's pastoral procedure generally.

Also in the 1850s a controversy was going on about the services at Porthleven. The incumbent had asked for funds to support his work there, and Canon Rogers, whose family had been benefactors of the church, objected to statements about the poverty of the original furnishings, and to the new parson's 'goings-on.' It appears there were between twenty and thirty candles around the altar on Easter Day, and a silver cross upon it, while banners were displayed during public worship. This attempt to bring brightness into the lives of the locals did not meet with the good Canon's approval, but the vicar, T. Lockyer Williams, found much support and the reverend Head Master of Ely Grammar School sprang to his aid with a pamphlet, *Ritual Beauty no Mark of Romanism.*

Nevertheless that is not what the public believed, but saw in the most innocent innovation the hidden hand of Rome. The more so, since in 1850 the new Roman hierarchy was appointed, and Plymouth became the seat of a Roman Catholic bishop. Great public resentment was aroused, and both sides agreed in venting their wrath upon the unfortunate men of the Oxford Movement, whom the protestants accused of being traitors and the papists as imitators.

The rector of Sheviock, like numbers of his brethren, found the struggle to disinter Prayer book truth too much for him. He was J. Somers Cocks, who in 1850 restored his chancel according to the rubric 'the chancels shall remain as they have done in times past'. At the opening there was a large gathering of clergy and others for the sung Eucharist, at which there was a celebrant, gospeller and epistoler. But the Church of England as a whole would not be hurried, and the difficulties became too much for Somers Cocks, who seceded to Rome in 1855.

Several among the clergy were moved to do the same

by the result of the Gorham controversy. George Cornelius Gorham was vicar of St. Just-in-Penwith, contentious and unpopular – 'He don't like we, and we don't like he' they said. In 1847 he was nominated to the Devon benefice of Bramford Speke. Phillpotts refused to institute him on the ground that he was unsound on baptismal doctrine. Gorham went to law, and carried his case to the Privy Council, who ruled Gorham's views were not cause for him to be refused institution. Some felt that the appeal to a secular court was the last straw and abandoned the Anglican Church. But the majority held firm and showed their loyalty. Phillpotts called a synod of his clergy and formally reaffirmed their faith in the formularies of the Church.

To many the innovators of ritual in the services seemed to be concerned with mere trivialities. But these things to them stood for principles, and though sometimes the new Tractarian vicar was unwise and hasty, he had a point – it was that the authority of the Church derives not from its State-favoured position, but from its apostolic foundation. But in fact, though the ritualist movement lay at the heart of the Revival, the new stirring was affecting many who would not share the Tractarian hopes. On all sides it was seen there was a need of bringing in order and dignity to the services and removing the slovenliness of the bad old days.

Everywhere the old church bands were going out, and the new organs and harmoniums were coming in, not without heartburning, as readers of Thomas Hardy's *Under the Greenwood Tree* – undoubtedly drawn from life – will remember. By 1895 there were 253 of these instruments, while 18 parishes still used a fairly complete band or some orchestral accompaniment. It is recorded that at Gunwalloe at the time of Marconi's pioneer wireless work in the vicinity, the great inventor attended service there. To help the music he paid a cornettist, as the player of the harmonium was, in local phrase, 'a poor whisht thing 'oo 'ardly 'ad strength to bla' the bellowses'!

The new choral arrangements also displaced the old metrical psalms so long in use in our churches. Collections of hymns had long been made in various parishes, but in 1861 the familiar *Ancient and Modern* appeared and quickly gained favour, though to some it was a dangerous Tractarian novelty. Local choral associations helped to raise standards of singing.

It was the desire of those in the forefront of the Revival that the services of the Church should be more frequently held, and that the times and nature of these services should be convenient to the parishioners. In place of the old morning prayer, litany, and ante-communion with a long sermon in the morning, and evening prayer and catechizing in the afternoon, the services were separated and the old quarterly communion, or monthly in the towns, was increased to at least a weekly Eucharist in several churches. By 1866 there was a weekly communion and a daily office at Antony, Carnmenellis, St. Columb Major, St. Ives, St. Mary's, and St. Paul's Penzance, Sheviock and St. Mary's Truro. After this the movement for more frequent service and for the churches to be open for prayer during the week spread widely, till today it is the norm in parishes of the most moderate sort of churchmanship.

There was a tremendous enthusiasm in the 1860s and 70s for the 'restoration' of churches. Hardly a building in the diocese escaped, for by that time there was a good deal of sheer ruin as a result of continuous neglect and centuries of hand-to-mouth repair. Among the architects whoso enjoyed the work of rebuilding and restoring were J. P. St. Aubyn, Gilbert Scott, G. E. Street, and J. Sedding. In 1872 Thomas Hardy restored St. Juliot and married the rector's sister. Knowledge and respect for old structures greatly increased toward the end of the century, though even today there is much to be desired in the quality of the furnishings of a mass-produced kind.

The general introduction of order, beauty and care of churches was made less contentious by the abolition in 1868 of the compulsory church rates. These had been levied on nonconformists and Churchmen alike, and the former not unnaturally resented the duty of supporting the parish church while they were contributing to their own place of worship. The abolition of the rate left the safety of the structure merely on 'an appeal to the sense of order and decency in every Congregation of Christian men'.

The general tidying up involved the putting-down of many irreverent but no doubt highly thought of customs. To the little church of St. Michael Caerhayes a new rector, William Willimot, was appointed in 1852. At the close of his first Sunday in the parish, noticing a light in the church, he went in, to find around the hideous stove which then stood in the very middle of the chancel, a group of men from the village sitting with hat on head, pipe in mouth, and a tankard in front of each! This 'ancient custom' was brought to an abrupt end! Himself a craftsman of skill, Willimot made some stained windows for Caerhayes church, but it was at Quethiock, to which parish he was appointed in 1878, that his best work was done. When he went to see the church there, rain was pouring in, and an umbrella had to be held over his head. Willimot got the church restored, and made with his own hands no less than nine windows, firing the glass in a little furnace on the vicarage lawn.

Towards the end of Phillpotts's occupancy of the see of Exeter we begin to discern the outlines of modern Church activity. The old casual eighteenth-century ways were being left behind. Rural chapters or synods for the clergy began in the 1840s. Pastoral letters from the bishop commended home and foreign missions, church building, and education. Many Church societies and organizations began. Work was opened up in new directions of social service, temperance, and among unmarried mothers with the founding of a home at Lostwithiel in 1861.

By 1859 no less than 163 Church schools were at work in 129 Cornish parishes, with 6,231 boys and 4,741 girls on the books. One effect of the better religious teaching was seen in the confirmations of the time. At Stratton in 1860 199 were confirmed, at St. Germans 131, at Penzance 298, and at other centres equally large numbers received the rite.

By far the most striking evidence of the revival of the Anglican Church in Cornwall in the nineteenth century is the dividing of the Exeter diocese and the presence of a bishop in Cornwall again. As far back as Cranmer's time it had been proposed to include a new bishopric with a seat at Bodmin, among others then being founded from the revenues of dissolved monastic houses. This scheme, however, fell through.

It was not until three hundred years later that the idea again became active. John Whitaker had sown a seed with his *Ancient Cathedral of Cornwall*, but it was slow to germinate. It was a realization of the impossibility of working the newly revivified archdeaconry from Exeter, with its different needs from those of Devon, which stirred in men's minds. Bishop Phillpotts himself with that forethought characteristic of him, retained a fifth canonry at Exeter at the time when cathedral establishments were being reduced to a dead level of four canonries in order to provide eventually for the start of a Cornish bishopric.

In 1847 a Bill was introduced for the foundation of four new sees, of which Cornwall was named as one with the bishop's seat at Bodmin. The choice of this town arose more from its old ecclesiastical importance and the survival of its magnificent parish church than from any real convenience as a centre. However, the Bill, introduced by Lord John Russell, came to nothing. A few years after this the bishop received the offer from Edmund Walker, rector of St. Columb Major, of the advowson of that wealthy benefice. This gift was either for the endowment of the bishopric or the foundation of canonries. Interest was shown in the proposal by the Cathedral Commission, and the Ecclesiastical Commissioners were approached for further augmentation of the proposed endowment, towards which Phillpotts himself was willing to forgo £500 of his income annually.

Enthusiastic meetings, many pamphlets and much propaganda stirred up increasing support, and a largely-signed memorial was presented in 1860 to Lord Palmerston by a deputation headed by the Earl of St. Germans. The names of Arthur Tatham, rector of Boconnoc, and Reginald Hobhouse, vicar of St. Ives, deserve to be remembered as able writers and tireless workers for the cause of the new see. However Palmerston was very casual about the affair and put the deputation off. Though the rebuff was the cause of great disappointment, the suggestion of utilizing St. Columb was not a wise one, as the town was remote and the church hardly of sufficient adequacy for a cathedral.

In the following years further unsuccessful attempts were made to get the government of the day to see the need for the Cornish see, the archbishop (Longley) himself coming down to the county to enable him to press the matter from an informed point of view. At this juncture bishop Phillpotts died, in 1869, to be followed by Frederick Temple, who took up his new position amid a certain amount of doubt and resentment, quickly dispelled, owing to his being a contributor to the volume *Essays and Reviews*.

His knowledge of the Church's need in the west assured him of the rightness of the proposal to divide the diocese, and this knowledge had been aided by devoted clergy and laity. Prebendary Tatham who had produced in 1850 a pamphlet, *A Cornish Bishopric; the Necessity and*

Means for its Restoration, had died in 1874. In 1869 the learned curate of St. Paul's, Truro, W. S. Lach-Szyrma, put out *A Letter to Mr. W. E. Gladstone,* setting forth the arguments in favour of the bishopric. Then a layman, Mr. Edmund Carlyon, came forward and brought the matter before the diocesan conference of 1874.

Dr. Temple saw there was no hope of persuading the State to recognize the claim of Cornwall to a share in the ancient endowments for the purpose of founding a new see. Funds would have to come from other sources. The bishop offered to surrender £800 of his own episcopal income and to hand over the patronage in Cornwall held by him as bishop. This offer was made at a great meeting held in Plymouth in March, 1875, and proved a tremendous stimulus. A committee was formed, and it was decided to send a deputation to the Prime Minister, Disraeli, the bishop himself heading it. Lady Rolle offered £40,000 conditional on the total sum needed being forthcoming. Subscriptions poured in, and within twelve months the committee was able to announce that the total required was available.

On 11th August, 1876 the necessary Act of Parliament for the foundation of the bishopric of Truro passed into law. The following year, Truro was raised to the dignity and style of a city, the parish church of Truro having been named in the Act as the cathedral church of the bishopric. The new diocese was to consist of the whole of Cornwall, the Scilly Isles, and five parishes on the Devon border. The archdeaconry of Bodmin was afterward created out of the eastern part of the county, the old title 'Archdeaconry of Cornwall' being retained for the west. It was announced in December 1876 that Edward White Benson, chancellor of Lincoln cathedral, had been chosen as the first bishop of Truro. He was a man who could understand and value the churchmanship of the different parties. His experience at Lincoln gave great promise that the new cathedral body would be organized on statutes which had been well tested.

Benson was consecrated at St. Paul's cathedral on St. Mark's day, 1877, by the archbishop of Canterbury and enthroned in St. Mary's, Truro on 1st May. It speedily became apparent that St. Mary's was completely inadequate as a cathedral, cramped and small as it was for diocesan functions. At the first diocesan conference held in the new diocese in November 1877 the matter of a new cathedral was mooted, and after much discussion a committee was appointed to consider what steps should be taken. The indefatigable Edmund Carlyon, secretary of the conference was also made secretary of the new building committee, the Earl of Mount Edgcumbe being chairman. Various proposals, a new building on a new site, the enlargement of St. Mary's, and a cathedral incorporating St. Mary's were all hotly argued in formal reports, newspaper letters, and on street corners. In August 1878 J. L. Pearson was engaged to prepare plans for the cathedral, being no stranger to Cornwall and responsible for some very beautiful modern churches. Very skilfully he retained the old south aisle of St. Mary's, with its splendid but decayed carved south front, and turned it into a second south aisle of the cathedral, where it remains as the parish church of Truro. The actual foundation stones of the new building were laid on Thursday, 20th May, 1880, by the Prince of Wales, afterwards Edward VII, in the presence of an immense throng of people.

With the beginning of building and the necessary structural alterations of the old church, a temporary wooden erection was brought into use to serve as a 'cathedral' until some portion of the new shrine was ready. By 1887 the choir and transepts, but not the nave, were completed and the consecration was carried out on 3rd November by Benson, then archbishop of Canterbury. The benediction of the nave followed in July, 1903, the central

Victoria tower in 1904, and the western towers and bells in 1910.

During the time of building the cathedral intense work had been going on to create the proper diocesan machinery and the necessary organizations. There had long been founded a Training College for Teachers at Truro, which had blossomed out in 1859 with new buildings after a period of struggle in private houses. There was of course at the turn of the century much controversy over education, the sharp cleavage between 'Board Schools' and 'Church Schools' finding additional flame by reason of nonconformist suspicion of church schools.

It was not long after Benson's arrival in Truro that he took the first steps to form a Theological College for the training of clergy for the diocese. But the term of usefulness of this venture was short; it came to an end in 1900 owing to the desire for previous university training and the drop in the numbers offering for holy orders.

To Benson the work of mission in the diocese was also a concern. Canon A. J. Mason was appointed as diocesan missioner, the first to hold such an office in the Church of England. That such work was necessary in Cornwall was evident. There was much misunderstanding of the Anglican position, much resentment of the new bishop and diocese existed among the ill-instructed, together with the ever-present need for plain Gospel preaching outside the walls of the churches. These missions won their way by the quiet sincerity of the missioner and his helpers. As early as the 1870s lay assistants, forerunners of the modern lay readers, were at work in the parishes, and laymen were associated with some of Mason's missions, as in the itinerant campaign of 1882 at St. Kew, St. Minver, and St. Endellion. As a result of these missions, many chapels of ease were built to serve outlying hamlets. In a single year, 1883, the second bishop, G. H. Wilkinson, presided at the opening of chapels at Washaway, Latchley and Zelah, blessed the rebuilt church of Temple, consecrated the new church at Looe, and laid the foundation of a new church at Redruth, while Mason preached at the founding of a new chapel at Carharrack!

The new bishop entered keenly into the multiplying activities of the new diocese. In his time the first stage of the cathedral was completed and consecrated, and the furnishing begun with gifts which poured in from diocese, parish, and individual donor within and without the county. Wilkinson was instrumental in bringing into being the Community of the Epiphany, a sisterhood or convent, of which the bishop is Visitor. Since its inception in 1883 the Community has had an untold influence and is a continuing spiritual force.

Among the 288 parochial clergy who ministered in the Cornish parishes in 1883 were men of excellence and learning. Such priests as Bush of Duloe, Wise of Ladock, Hullah of Calstock, Hockin of Phillack – widely known as an authority on Methodism – Chappel of Camborne, and others, stayed on in their parishes, knew and ruled their people, provided schools and other buildings out of their own pockets, and have left their mark on their parishes to this day.

With the approach of the twentieth century the Church in Cornwall was in the midst of what may be judged to be its most prosperous period. It had been an act of faith, as well as of employment to embark upon building schemes of the magnitude of a cathedral, and the founding of new churches and schools, since distress and unemployment had been caused by the collapse of the mines in the 1870s and the emigration of many Cornishmen to seek work abroad.

It was at this time that churchgoing was at its height of fashion. The security of village life, revolving around the 'big house' and the rectory with its trim garden seemed permanent. Year succeeded year like the slow ticking of an

ancient clock. There was the sound of the parson's dog-cart
in the dusty lane, the harvest tea on the vicarage lawn, the
servants, the sense of 'proper station'. Symbolic of this
permanence was the long span as vicar of Gulval of William
Wingfield – a sick man, instituted in 1839, he lived on to
serve his people for 73 years as parish priest, ending his days
just on the threshold of the first world war and the break-up
of the old order, in 1912.

Nevertheless there were beneath the surface tensions
and impending change even before. It was a Cornishman,
John William Colenso, born at St. Austell in 1814, who as
missionary and bishop in Natal voiced the principles of
Biblical criticism in his commentary on the Pentateuch
(1862–5), and stirred up a tremendous controversy which
was one of the facets of the Victorian battle between
'science' and 'religion'. There were many who felt that the
limits of deviation from the Prayer book were too strait,
and that Tractarian gains in proclaiming the Church
'Catholic' as well as 'Reformed' did not go far enough.
Some wished to approximate the Anglican services to those
of continental Rome. Such a one was Sandys Wason, vicar
of Cury, who in 1910 brought on himself the censure of the
bishop, Stubbs. At length the parishioners took the matter
into their own hands, and there ensued the tragicomedy
of Wason's eviction from the vicarage. But the problem
remained – how far in any direction should liberty be
allowed in departing from the services of a book compiled
in 1662? Bishop Burroughs held a synod of his clergy in
1914 to debate this matter; the rumblings of Prayer book
revision began to be heard.

The continuing industrial difficulties and disputes
were reflected in the life of the Church. For instance in
the clayworkers' strike in 1913 there was concern in the
bishop's letters and prayers in the churches. There was also
a sense of gravity at the troubles in Ireland, and a sympathy
with the Welsh Church in its impending disestablishment.

The outbreak of war in 1914 turned the activity of the diocese into unwonted directions. Soon there were exhortations on duty in time of war, prayer for the homeless, the wounded, and the fallen. Churches, which had in many places been closed except on Sundays, remained open for private prayer. Requiems were offered in the cathedral from 1915 onwards and in an increasing number of parishes. Members of Fowey Church of England Men's Society established a recreation hut at St. Anthony, for the servicemen stationed there, and other plans for help and relief were put in hand.

The monthly notes of bishop Burroughs reflect the gravity of the war situation. Nevertheless the Church was thinking ahead to the peace. Already many were trying to devise ways of giving greater freedom to the Church to order her affairs without legal trammels, to find new ways of worship, and to allow the laity their due share in Church government. A diocesan financial scheme came into operation to augment poor livings and to begin the provision of pensions for clergy. The reconciliation of modern thought and religious belief – a perennial subject – and the rise of the 'Modernist' school gave anxiety to many older clergy. Of the 270 clergy at work in the diocese in 1918, 161 were over 51.

After the war a noticeable decline in church attendance began, due in part possibly to the shattering of faith in the comfortable ideas of the inevitability of progress, and in the easy 'Christianity' of the time. But deepening spirituality had come to many as a result of the bitter times they had passed through, and there began a marked rise in the number of communions made in many parishes. Reflecting this was the resolution before the diocesan conference of 1919 that the Eucharist should be the chief service of Sunday devotions.

All the machinery which it was hoped would lead to a freer Church as a result of the 'Enabling Act' of 1919 was put into motion during the course of 1920 and succeeding years under the guidance of the new bishop, Guy Warman. A great morality campaign in Cornwall was well supported, while the trend towards easier divorce found many ready to protest. Other results of war were plain in the prevailing unemployment in Cornwall, poverty, and economic instability. The mining areas around Camborne, Redruth and St. Just were badly hit by the closing down of many mines which had survived earlier setbecks.

Faced with this many clergy tended to move leftward in their political views, seeing in Christian socialism the true expression of the Gospel in the affairs of this world. Frank Fincham, curate of St. Paul's, Truro, 'Monty' May of Torpoint, and above all Jack Bucknall, priest-in-charge of Delabole were men who preached and tried to live out this interpretation of Christ's teaching. Others promoted work for the unemployed, and Ladd-Canney of Pencoys, later Redruth, identified himself with the miners' cause and toured with their choir in an attempt to focus public concern on their plight. Social service, moral welfare, temperance work and the like, which had long been a care of the Church in the diocese, received added support. In the wider concerns, the persecution of Russian churchmen, and the League of Nations, were constantly pressed as subjects for Christian prayer.

Country parishes, small in population and in stipend, became even more of a problem owing to the reduced numbers of clergy to staff them, and the absence of private means among them. Joining up of parishes began, the large parsonages became emptier of servants and burdensome to repair, though the new dilapidations measure in 1923 relieved the worst cases. The parishes of Broadwoodwidger and St. Germansweek, two parishes in Devon originally included in the new diocese of Truro, were taken back into the Exeter diocese in 1922, being too remote from the see city in west Cornwall.

When bishop Warman announced his translation to Chelmsford in 1923 the bishops welcomed the promotion to their number of one who was universally recognized as being in the front rank of liturgical scholars. Walter Frere however was a member of the Community of the Resurrection, now widely honoured but then viewed with protestant suspicion by the old-fashioned. Enthroned in November 1923 Frere made it clear that though he was commonly regarded as a 'ritualist' it was the spiritual and moral state of the diocese for which he cared most. He recognized good work where he saw it, though perhaps it might not be done as he would wish. For instance the priests at Delabole (Bucknall) and St. Hilary (Walke) were individualists – the one politically of the Thaxted type of Christian socialist, the other completely Latin in theology and practice. Both had great followings, and from St. Hilary came some of the first broadcast nativity plays, of moving simplicity. Both men were bitterly opposed by the conservative gentry, but Frere never forgot that work was being done which no-one else could do, and would not support the opposition.

In his time encouragement was given to work among the homeless and the down-and-out. Basil Jellicoe, founder of the St. Pancras Housing Society stirred much interest in the county, and the Franciscans of Cerne Abbas opened up work among wayfarers at Bodrean in St. Clement, which carried on until the threshold of the recent war.

Stirred to a keen interest in the relics of the Celtic past Frere encouraged Cornish studies, and himself led the first diocesan pilgrimage to St. Piran's Oratory in 1924, as an act of worship and of recognition of the ancient culture remaining in the county. He drew around him friends, such as Charles Henderson, whose *Cornish Church Guide* (1925) is still the envy of other dioceses and whose interest in Cornish studies has placed a multitude in his debt. There was also Gilbert Doble, vicar of Wendron 1925–45, to whom we owe those painstaking researches which have rehabilitated the study of our Christian forefathers, and many another who found encouragement from Frere. The width of the bishop's interests was seen in the visit paid to his cathedral in 1925 by Russian prelates, who turned to him as to a brother when in England.

Of a different order was the rule of his successor, Joseph Wellington Hunkin, son of a Truro merchant who was a Methodist preacher of the old school. Hunkin gave intellectual stimulus to many who did not find his churchmanship congenial, and his friendliness won many hearts. Not long after his enthronement the country was at war again, and the unexpected sight of a bishop in Home Guard uniform was soon usual in Truro. Hunkin had been a well-loved chaplain in the first war, and was eager to associate the Church of England with the defence of the country.

Evacuees poured into the county, among them the boys of cathedral choir schools such as Canterbury and St. Paul's. Most villages received large numbers of young people, and many pastoral opportunities and some problems resulted, To not a few of the evacuees it was the first contact they had had with the Church and lasting impressions were made. Some churches in the eastern parts of the county were damaged – Torpoint, Botus Fleming, Saltash St. Nicholas – but it was mostly slight and soon repaired. A keenly-felt casualty of the time was the closing of the Truro Training College in 1938–9 through economic troubles; it was an irreparable loss to the diocese and the county.

To Hunkin's friendliness, taking advantage of the growing nearness of war, and his acceptability as a thorough Cornishman, may be attributed the breakthrough against ecclesiastical prejudice. He set men thinking out their position as churchmen, and got them talking together. He brought together churchmen and nonconformists, and old suspicions began to be sloughed off, while the real divisions became clearer in consequence. His successor, Edmund Morgan, quickly won the affection and respect of Cornishmen, including many leading Methodists. He found it profitable to bring Methodists and churchmen together for conversations on unity, and to work with the former closely without sacrifice of principle. A considerable flowering of activity in adult and youth education has resulted, jointly undertaken. Under his guidance the building of new churches, in the very different conditions of today, has gone on with churches and halls at Kenwyn, Wadebridge, Trevone and Penwerris, worthy to take their place alongside the other churches built earlier in the twentieth century, such as Newquay, Falmouth All Saints', Camelford and Carbis Bay.

Today the Church of England in the diocese, presided over by the present bishop, John Maurice Key, is active in its work, faithful in its beliefs, and loyal in its practice, though it may gather fewer numbers than at the beginning of the century. It is served by 211 clergy, of whom 200 are incumbents taking charge of 221 parishes with the help of 49 diocesan and 48 parochial lay readers. The official basis of membership in the Anglican Church is the Easter communion number, and this stands at about 28,000 out of a population of 346,871 in Cornwall.

While there are of course differences in churchmanship in the diocese, party feeling does not now run high, and the prevailing tone is one of sober views with very few extremes on either hand. On occasion there will be friendly co-operation with the local Methodists or other Christian groups, and there are many who are hopeful that the continuing talks on the subject of unity with the Methodists will, if nothing else, lead to greater understanding of one another's viewpoint.

Church activities are far too numerous to mention individually, but worthy of notice is the Mothers' Union with 118 branches and 3,536 members. The Community of the Epiphany, in fruitful harness with the local authority, runs a convalescent home at St. Agnes, and a rest home for elderly folk at Rosewin, Truro. The diocese maintains support of its schools, of which there are 54 with aided status, giving full Church access, and 26 controlled schools. The Cathedral School and the High School provide a grammar and public school education, and at Penzance St. Clare's School (for girls) is a Woodard foundation. There is a considerable degree of co-operation with the Roman Catholic Church and the Free Churches in the matters of education and moral welfare.

Large sums are raised annually for diocesan and central funds, and for the repair of church fabric which is now subject to a quinquennial inspection by an architect, as are parsonage houses. At the same time missionary giving is increasing and the familiar societies of the Church of England are well supported.

Of course the problems are numerous and testing. There is the task, not confined to Cornwall, of commending the Gospel in terms suitable to a technically-trained generation including at the same time many of simpler outlook. There is the innate conservatism of people in the far west, who resist change and are indifferent to abstract principles, but who readily respond to friendship. Pastoral problems arise from the shortage and age of clergy, and the necessary pluralities which render pastoral contact less immediate. Shifts of population have left some churches isolated and in bad repair, while rising costs of putting things right fall heavily on the minority. Spiritual isolation and lack of incentive to intellectual advance is often the lot of clergy in moorland parishes and lonely villages. But in the wisdom and light which come through faith these and similar problems are being faced.

Epilogue

WITH SWEEPING GLANCE THE WHOLE SPAN OF THE CHURCH'S history in the county has been taken in. It is a story of rise and fall, of faithfulness and worldly pride. It is a story of unity and of fragmentation, of apparently imminent death and of astonishing revival.

There will be some who can discern no plan or shape in such a story, pointing to the rise of divisions and parties, with bitterness and clamour hiding devotion and spiritual awareness.

What plan or shape there is will be discovered by the reader according to his faith.

To the believer the purposes of God patiently and faithfully unfold in history. And that is the justification for the telling of this story.

Index

Abbot-bishops, 18
Algar, prior of Bodmin, 35
Appropriations, 35
Athelstan, 28
Articles of Rebels, 60
Atwell, Hugh, 69
Arianism among Dissenters, 113
Arundells, 41, 60, 104, 106

Bells, 58, 61, 96, 145
Benson, Edward White, bishop of Truro, 143f
Black Death, 43
Bodmin, Gospels, 24
  priory, 21
  relics of St. Petroc, 40
Borlase, Walter, 89
Bray, William, 85
  Billy, 128
Bronescombe, Walter, bishop of Exeter, 38, 42

Cathedral, Exeter, 34
  Truro, 141
Catholic Recusants, 67
Catholic Revival in Anglican Church, 135, 136
Celtic features, 22f

  saints, 17f
Chantries, 48
  property, 49, 56
  suppression, 56
Classis, Cornwall, 72
Colenso, John William, bishop of Natal, 147
Commonwealth, 71
Conan, Saxon bishop of St. Germans, 28

Danes, 27
Deprivations, papal clergy, 64
  Anglican clergy, 72
  Puritans, 111
Dissolution of monasteries, 55
Dumnonii, 12, 26

Eadulf, bishop of Crediton, 27
Egbert, 27
Elizabeth I, religious changes under, 64
  excommunication, 66
Estates, episcopal, 27
Exeter Assembly, 112
Exeter, seiges of, 51

Falmouth Church, 79
Fingar, or Gwinear, St., 14, 15

157